ANGELS

The Guardians of Your Destiny

by
Maiya and Geof Gray-Cobb

Library of Congress Cataloging-in-Publication Data
Gray-Cobb, Maiya. 1929 -, Gray-Cobb, Geof 1928 -
"Angels - The Guardians of Your Destiny"
by Maiya and Geof Gray-Cobb
This angel book takes you on fascinating and rewarding mental journeys into a world of heavenly beings.
1. Ancient History 2. Archeology 3. Lost Civilizations
4. Extraterrestrials
I. Gray-Cobb, Maiya 1929 - II. Gray-Cobb, Geof 1928- III. Title

Library of Congress Catalog Number: 2007941101
ISBN: 978-1-886940-78-9
Cover Art and Layout by www.enki3d.com
Book Design: Julia Degan
Book Set in: Times New Roman, Monotype Corsiva, Parchment

Published by

OZARK
MOUNTAIN
PUBLISHING
PO Box 754
Huntsville, AR 72740

www.ozarkmt.com
Printed in the United States of America

Maiya and I had intended to write this book together. Just after she got started, I had the misfortune to have heart and stroke attacks and so far, I haven't written a word of it. I gave her lots of encouragement instead and carried out the spell check for her which is why my name is also on the book. Having read it, I realize I have neither the ability nor the spiritual knowledge that Maiya has. If you enjoy this one, and I did, you'll find the sequel called "The Seeds of the Soul" is even more fascinating.

Geof Gray-Cobb

Dedication

To Julia and her team: Thanks for a splendid and dedicated piece of work.

TABLE OF CONTENTS

Introduction

Do Angels really exist? Certainly they exist - come with us and we'll show you that Angels are many and varied but all of them are specialized energies of intelligence and they can help you in amazing ways

INTRODUCTION

What is an Angel? Are there really such things?

In this book, you will enter their mystic world through exploring the deep waters of folklore, myth and legend; yet emerge safely onto the dry land of reality and truth; giving you a wide-ranging perception of how to become a practical and practicing celestial initiate of the Inner Worlds that surround us in which these Angels exist.

So where do we start? Well, most people know that Angels watch over us and help to keep us from harm. But the very first Angel you're likely to have heard about is your own Guardian Angel, the one who watches over you. Allegory describes how this particular Angel appears as you are being born, and your soul is being guided into your body. From there on in your Angel stays with you, looking after you in a multitude of ways.

Then, apart from your personal Angel, accounts of other Angels helping, speaking, appearing, even warning us of dangers have been handed down from the mists of time.

Far in the past, in the Bible, we read how Hagar, Manoah and Mary were all visited by a tattletale Angel who announced their pregnancies, apparently before the women themselves knew about their blessed events.

And, inevitably, we come across the Angel Lucifer, the Light Giver, who seems to have really gotten a raw deal when God kicked him out of Heaven with some of his associates just because they got a bit too self-important. Lucifer disagreed with the orders he was given and refused to carry them out, and ultimately got himself a really bad reputation.

Or you can think of the Angel of Glory, Sandalphon, so named for his love of sandals. We're told he was originally the prophet Elijah in his earthly incarnation, while the Cabala, the mystic theosophy of the Hebrews, reports that Sandalphon has the task of selecting the sex of babies while they're in the embryonic stage. That's a useful angelic factor for expectant mothers to know, although Sandalphon must work hand-in-hand with ultrasound and the Angel Azrael, frequently called the Angel of death.

Azrael's chief task is to record in the pages of an immense book the names of those who have just been born, and also to erase the names of the newly dead. This data is then passed on to the appropriate celestial plane. Azrael is the Angel most often described when a family member or close friend goes to his or her demise, being shepherded safely by a Seraph.

Joseph, husband of Mary and father of Jesus was also warned by an Angel of the wrath of Herod, and they were able to escape into Egypt.

Then coming further up the time line into the 1800's, Joseph Smith, the founder and first prophet of the Mormon Church, claimed he received the gold plates of hieroglyphics of the Book of Mormon from the hands of the Angel Moroni. Using magic spectacles supplied by the Angel, Smith and Moroni transcribed the text, but although Moroni was a good translator he clearly wasn't a true Guardian Angel: a disorderly mob who allegedly detested Smith's plural marriage decree, murdered him in 1844.

Even later, during the last two world wars, many service people who were in pain or dying have told of their experiences and encounters with Angels. One of the most famous Angelic advents was in the First World War during the retreat from Mons in 1914. A report was published that spectral bowmen were taking souls of the dead up to the Pearly Gates. The

Angels, who appeared as sword-brandishing saviors on horseback, were witnessed by their living comrades.

But myth and legend notwithstanding, lately more and more Angels have been seen and experienced in one form or another. Is our awareness of the Inner Worlds of the Unseen becoming more acute? Are we answering the call from the Beings of Light who are searching for those who are ready to become Initiates? Are the budding Initiates, searching for the beginning of The Path, meeting their guides in the form of Angels?

The answer to these questions is here as we come back to that original question: What is an Angel?

According to author Crawford H. Greenewalt, your average Angel weighs in the region of 150 lbs (about 68 kg.) with wings each roughly 4 feet (1.2 meters) from wrist to tip. Earlier ideas suggested that Angels have feathered wings and don't need to flap them: Angels thoughts and desires speed them any distance without this effort.

First, disregard the wings and feathers - they appeared around the 17th century when the Church decided that anything that flew like an Angel obviously had to have wings. But keep the idea that Angels can move from place to place using thought alone.

Angels are actually specialized energies of intelligence, each with their own duties to perform, yet they work together as a group even if you only meet one. You see, no single energy is capable of performing at warp speed, so when an Angel is called upon to perform a particular activity, the remainder of the group adds their energies to the one called upon. Usually, there's a leader of any particular group and the Angels work under this organizer and their built-in intelligence is shared by them all.

Myriad energies flow within the Astral Planes and should you decide to follow the Path of the Initiate, you will be gradually introduced to these forces as you mentally travel from one level of consciousness to another within the Planes. These Angel energies will help in many ways to guide you along your chosen path of destiny.

Your first and foremost assignment will be to find your personal Angel group, which contains your Guardian Angel, by following the instructions in Chapter 1.

Next, before you actually make contact with your Angel group, you'll get to know and empower yourself by making a personal profile of your inner and outer being. As you carry out this work, you'll meet your Angels, develop a mental health ledger, make a dream diary, set up your goals and learn how to keep track of personal changes as you discover and begin to access your inner resources.

The Path gets a little steeper from Chapter 5 onward and there you get a choice: you can either gather your courage and take the Mind Walk to enter a world of wonders, or you can remain as you are and be satisfied with your share of the world as you know it.

But having made your choice to walk the Path, your journey really begins from the start of Chapter 6.

And there's more to come. The remainder of this book is not for the faint of heart. Once you've taken the inevitable first step, you will be expected to work hard, with dedication, and you will be tested time and time again. You will need faith and acceptance to explore the realms of Angels and Beings of Light. But most of all you will need bravery to face yourself first, to cross that perilous, sinister place which is the dark side of your Inner Self, where you will face your own demons.

This is the place of journeys and memories. You have to be unfaltering and steadfast to travel through to the Other Side. Once you have accomplished this, you are on the threshold of proving yourself worthy of becoming an Initiate.

Other chapters will lead you higher and higher through level after level, taking you to the Mystical Door whose key you will turn as you reach for the Infinite.

Where will *your* journey take *you*? Fate alone will answer that question, but know that there are many fascinating Beings waiting to greet you, and you can find out only by putting one foot in front of the other and see where you end up.

Shall we let the journey begin?

The First Great Virtue of those who seek
the Spiritual Path
is courage .

Chapter 1
Finding your own personal Angels

he Angel group we mentioned earlier which was given to you when you were born is not just a random choice. The way the group is gathered together depends on your birthday. And that's a most important time as it indicates your life path this time around the wheel. Oh, yes – you'll find reincarnation in this context, along with many other metaphysical ideas.

As far as your birthday and your Angel group is concerned, there are six items to check off:

1. The date of your birth
2. The month of your birth
3. The sign of the zodiac
4. The ruler of that sign
5. The day of your birth
6. The hour of your birth

These data have been celestially selected with great care and attention to your needs. By checking out these facts of your life, you will find you already have six Angels lined up for your attention plus the head honcho under whose direction these Angels will function. That, by simple arithmetic, makes a celestial group of seven around you.

All these details have been very carefully worked out in the Inner Planes for you long before you were born. In fact, even though you don't recall it, you were there at a round table discussion along with the Angels of the Akashic Record and the Lords of Karma, whom you will meet in later chapters.

The first order of business was to check the Akashic Record to view your previous lives to see what good deeds you carried out in the past and also what bad seeds you sowed which will need accounting for in lives to come.

Next, the Lords of Karma got into the picture by explaining your previous experiences and your reactions to them. Then they told you what else you have to work through in the way of karmic obligations. Having carefully consulted with these wise Supreme Beings and selected your experiences for the life your soul is about to take on, you are now shown a variety of parents through whom you will get the start of your experiences.

When you have finally made your choice, the die is cast, Azrael writes your name and gender in his book of souls about to be born along with all the birth data.

Once you've made your decision to reincarnate, you have plenty of time to consider how you will handle your new life. You've had plenty of advice from the Lords of Karma regarding your actions and reactions to your new environment and the people within it. You have been told that a negative response such as criticism, lack of patience, corrosive thoughts or guilt, builds future Karma keeping you to the Wheel for further incarnations. Whereas giving harmony, love, understanding and peace to others helps towards canceling karmic debts. Don't worry about this right now, we'll explain the ramifications of positive and negative responses in much more detail in the following chapters when you make the profile of yourself.

But let's get back to your soul for a moment. When do you personally, actually take up residence in your new physical temple? It's done in stages, or layers if you will, although there is no actual "fixed" moment.

When your future mother was about six months pregnant, your soul started its gradual descent towards your Inner Temple. A portion of your soul progressively took up residence with more and more arriving until at the moment of birth some ninety percent was within bounds of your body.

The remaining ten percent kept a toehold in the Planes for as long as ten days after your birth, and gradually became assimilated by your grosser physical temple. However, if the soul feels it has made an error in its choice and wishes to reverse its decision against staying in physical and living form, that ten percent is able to "wind in" the rest of itself as it quits the earth plane and returns to the Inner Planes.

Actually, the soul never *completely* enters the body. A portion, a minuscule portion, remains between the earth plane and the Inner Planes which forms what is called the Astral (or silver) cord; also mentioned in the Bible in Ecclesiastes 12, 6-7, "Before the silver cord is scrapped and the Spirit returns to God who gave it". This cord ensures that when the soul leaves the body during the sleep state, it can get reeled in at the waking stage (or if anything disturbs the sleeping body).

Now, during this time, your group of Angels have been with you all the way guiding your every move. And at the final appropriate moment, usually with much heartache and many tears, saying farewell to a beautiful place of love and warmth, you drink of the waters of forgetfulness which erases the memory of where you have just come from. Here is the start of your new life and your Angels will always be there to help and guide you.

Now we come to the equation of how to find your group of

Angels. Remember the six steps mentioned earlier? Here are two examples of how it works. And when you understand how it is done, you will use your own personal data and select your Angels from the lists which follow the examples.

Let's say you were born on the 9th July (the year is not necessary).Check the lists on the following pages as we do each step.

#1: the date of birth   =   9th   = Angel Azar
#2: the month of birth   =   July = Angel Imrief
#3: the zodiac sign   =   Cancer = Angel Cael
#4: the ruler of the sign =   Moon = Angel Pi-Jo
#5: the day of birth   =   Friday = Angel Sarabotes
#6: the time of birth   =   3.27 p.m.Angel Parmiel

This makes up your group of six and the head Angel under whom they work is Angel Vequaniel, whose name you will find in the list of times of birth for 3p.m. You do not need the exact time, on the hour is just fine because the Angels rule from one hour to the next. Did you follow that one?

Here's another example for a November 16th birth.

#1: date of birth   = 16th   = Angel Madin
#2: the month   = November = Angel Ahadiss
#3: zodiac sign   = Scorpio   = Angel Riehol
#4: ruler of the sign = Pluto   = Angel Ambriel
#5: day of birth   = Wednesday = Angel Miel
#6: time of birth   = 2a.m.   = Angel Praxil

The head Angel under whom these work is Farris, found under the list of times of birth for 2a.m.

Now, get yourself a sheet of paper and pencil, or boot up your computer and select a suitable memo program such as Notepad or

WordPad. Record your own data as shown in the examples and then fill in your own Angels from the lists below following each step from 1 to 7.

Here in step 1 are the Angel names of the numbered days.

1st	Lahabiel	16th	Madin
2nd	Ahariel	17th	Diniel
3rd	Samael	18th	Ygail
4th	Shahriva	19th	Adroni
5th	Valnum	20th	Miton
6th	Anael	21st	Veruah
7th	Ahiel	22nd	Jesod
8th	Sadquiel	23rd	Neciel
9th	Azar	24th	Sadayal
10th	Aban	25th	Todros
11th	Johiel	26th	Astad
12th	Seth	27th	Tufiel
13th	Tir	28th	Sebastien
14th	Katspiel	29th	Alesimus
15th	Tatriel	30th	Miniel
		31st	Astel

Now, having found the name of your date Angel and written it down, move to step 2.

Here are the Angels which match to your month of birth. Careful here: the months match the signs of the zodiac not from the beginning of the month to the end. The astrological month starts around the 20th to 22nd, and the zodiac year begins around the third week of March. So watch your dates carefully.

March 21-April 20 :	Favardin
April 21-May 20 :	Asmodel
May 21-June 20 :	Leybel
June 21-July 20 :	Imrief

5

July 21-Aug 20 :   Afsi-Khof
Aug 21-Sept 20 :   Morael
Sept 21-Oct 20 :   Elogium
Oct 21-Nov 20 :   Ahadiss
Nov 21-Dec 20 :   Ophiel
Dec 21-Jan 20 :   Nadiel
Jan 21-Feb 20 :   Ausiel
Feb 21-Mar 20 :   Isfandarmend

Following your month Angel, you come to step 3 where you find your Angel who rules your zodiac sign. If you really don't know what your zodiac sign is, your friendly astrologer will be able to tell you. Ask him or her what your Sun Sign is - it means the same as your zodiac sign.

The Angels ruling your zodiac sign are:

Aries: Malahidael
Taurus: Bagdal
Gemini: Sariel
Cancer: Cael
Leo: Verchiel
Virgo: Iadara
Libra: Zaniel
Scorpio: Riehol
Sagittarius: Sarataiel
Capricorn: Haniel
Aquarius: Archer
Pisces: Rasamasa

So having established your Angel ruling your zodiac sign, you move to step 4. Each sign is ruled by one of the planets in our solar system and each planet has a ruling Angel. Below are listed the Angels of the planets, and we've included the zodiac sign in case you do not know which planet rules which sign.

6

Planet	Sign Ruled	Ruling Angel
Mars	Aries	Ertosi
Venus	Taurus	Eurabatrus
Mercury	Gemini	Pi-Hermes
Moon	Cancer	Pi-Joh
Sun	Leo	Pi-Re
Mercury	Virgo	Arista
Venus	Libra	Hagith
Pluto	Scorpio	Ambriel
Jupiter	Sagittarius	Zachariel
Saturn	Capricorn	Kafziel
Uranus	Aquarius	Azel
Neptune	Pisces	Joel

Step 5 tabulates the Angels who rule the days of the week. On which day were you born? Then choose:

Sunday:	Hurtapal	Thursday:	Sachiel
Monday:	Curaneil	Friday:	Sarabotes
Tuesday:	Hyniel	Saturday:	Machatan
Wednesday:	Miel		

Now step 6 gives you the Angels who rule the time of day you were born. While step 7 names the chief Angel under whom each group works.

7

If you were born at:	Your hour Angel is:	Your chief Angel is:
1:00 am	Arathiel	Gamiel
2:00 am	Praxil	Farris
3:00 am	Crucial	Sarquamich
4:00 am	Phorsiel	Jefischa
5:00 am	Patrozin	Abasdarhon
6:00 am	Prenostix	Zaazonash
7:00 am	Anapion	Mendrion
8:00 am	Hanoziz	Gastrion
9:00 am	Adrapen	Nacoriel
10:00 am	Mameroijud	Jusquarin
11:00 am	Adjuchas	Dardariel
Noon	Darmosiel	Sarandiel
1:00 pm	Charmeas	Soluzen
2:00 pm	Labezerin	Anael
3:00 pm	Parmiel	Vequaniel
4:00 pm	Aclahaye	Vachmiel
5:00 pm	Camasayar	Sazqhiel
6:00 pm	Medussusiel	Samil
7:00 pm	Librabis	Barquiniel
8:00 pm	Iphun	Oscaebiel
9:00 pm	Kirtabus	Vadriel

10:00 pm	Chorob	Oriel
11:00 pm	Rosabis	Bariel
Midnight	Voizia	Beratiel

Careful when you use this list. If you are born in the morning use the a.m. list, from noon onwards use the p.m. list. If you have followed the steps 1 through 7 as we've indicated, you'll end up with your group of seven Angels who have helped to start off your destiny.

You started your life with seven personal Angels who will be around and with you constantly. As you climb the spiritual ladder, you will meet and become involved with many more Angel energies who will guide and lift your soul energy to the next level of accomplishment. Meanwhile, let's investigate the interesting theory of numbers which is said to be the basis of the Universe. Pythagoras backs this up stating that "the world is built upon the power of numbers".

Chapter 2
Numbers are Important

aving established your personal seven Angels, you might wonder why there are, in fact, seven of them. Why not just one Angel? The simple answer is that a single Angel, although pretty omnipotent, just doesn't have the necessary power and energy requirements to carry the full load of your manifest destiny. For good metaphysical reasons, that you'll recognize as you explore each chapter of this book, this has to be a group involvement. So while we're latched onto this seven business, we might as well investigate it more fully.

Seven is, and has always been, a magical number. From time immemorial, seven has had the reputation for mysterious and extraordinary power. Seven often appears in occult charms and spells, and the number is tied into numerous myths and superstitions, such as the suggestion that any child who is the seventh born has magical and clairvoyant powers. And if you can find the seventh child of a seventh child that individual is ultimately powerful and can, among other accomplishments, heal the sick. And talking about children, the goddess Hathor, who loved babies, was protectress of infants in arms. She had a group of seven goddesses who assisted her in her nursing activities and these seven also played the part of fairies around the cradle of newborn babes.

Seven pops up all over the place. Count the colors of the rainbow, there are seven of those. Further along in this text you'll meet the Lords of the Seven Rays, and that's an awe-inspiring side issue all by itself. Sound the notes of music: in western parlance at least, there are seven tones which have been recognized in some metaphysical disciplines as soul notes. The original seven planets which we have been using in the previous chapter, are known as the spheres of space. And the seven chakras, or spiritual focal points, of the human body form a nucleus (the hub) of Eastern teachings in relation to the Universe and its spirituality. And on a more intimate level, did you know that our bodies have seven channels of elimination? In several other traditions, the Cosmos is believed to consist of seven planes of existence.

Then, when you have a multiple seven, things really start to happen. For instance, in holy writ we have the story of how Joshua seized the city of Jericho. He hired seven priests who had seven trumpets and Joshua told them to march around the city walls once a day for six days. Then on the seventh day the priests marched around seven times and on the seventh go round they blew a long blast on their seven trumpets, and the walls simply fell down. Another multiple from Revelation 21:9 states, "And there came unto me one of the seven angels which had the seven vials full of the seven last plagues".

A special dream that Pharaoh had abounds in sevens: fat cows, lean cows, plump ears of corn and blighted ones all resonate to the mystic number. As does the Book of Revelations which has groups of sevens: stars, Angels, plagues and trumpets to name but a few. Namaan the leper washed seven times in the river Jordan and was healed. The Book of Proverbs refers to the seven pillars of wisdom. Then somewhere along the line the seven deadly sins were born: pride, lust, envy, avarice, wrath, greed and laziness which became cause for churchly penance. And to balance up the sins came the seven virtues of justice, prudence, temperance, fortitude, faith, hope and love, although the last named somehow got its name changed to charity. And for a final one-upmanship the church added in the seven sacraments and the seven sorrows of the Virgin Mary.

Across the Mediterranean, the Jewish religion set aside Saturday, the seventh day, as their day of rest. Mosaic law suggests the Sabbath (from the Hebrew shabbath – rest) to be a sacred time-out as do the Seventh Day Adventists, but the Christian Church chose Sunday which they call the Lords Day.

Leviticus follows the seven routine: that book says that every seven years the land should have a Sabbatical year of solemn rest to recuperate from its hard labors and the people were required to refrain from tillage, a custom handed down from ancient Jews. Biblically, the number seven is universal, but long before the writers of the holy books appropriated their information from earlier writings and then rewrote them to suit their particular cultures and outlook, their predecessors were already well aware of the power of the number. They knew instinctively that the key to this number was actually connected with significant periods of time stemming from links to our satellite, the Moon.

Think about the Moon as it grows to its perfect rounded glory at Full Moon and then dies to a slim crescent just before New Moon, ready to be born and shine its full light again. Now consider the cycles of life and death, (the coming and going) also the growth and decay on earth which are linked to the waxing and waning of the Moon. These four phases (and four is another very powerful number we'll be discussing shortly) are each of seven days duration. And that's the basis of our month of four weeks, each week being seven days. If you add together all the numbers from one to seven you'll find they total 28, the days of a lunar month, reinforcing the connection of seven with the lunar cycle.

Occultists and astrologers have long known that the rhythms of earth life run in periods of seven, corresponding to the rhythms of the Moon. For instance, the human menstruation cycle – all life depends on this event – occurs in a cycle of four by seven - that's every 28 days, each period lasting about three and a half days (half of seven).

Every seven years is an important step in life, rarely noticed unless you're into astrology or psychology. During the first seven you learn about life from parents and other family members. How your mind was structured during this period determines your actions and reactions to life at a later date when you have to make your own decisions within the social milieu. The growth of life - the learning and understanding - takes place within the first four periods of seven years (that's 28 years). By the time you're 56 (another 28 years) you can recognize how you've applied this knowledge to life's experiences, gaining awareness of your actions and reactions (your karmic choices) to these episodes. How many times have we heard older people say, "I wish I knew then what I know now, things might be different." But if we have made our own karmic choices before we were born, wouldn't we experience them one way or another, no matter what our decisions, when or how?

So what's all this got to do with your group of seven Angels? Well, apart from being with you throughout your life, they guide you through each of the seven year critical key points in your life. And also as you traverse the four levels of the Inner Planes, should you decide to walk the Path of the Initiate.

These four levels are the physical, mental, creative and archetypal levels. During chapters 1 to 4 we will be working with the physical or first level, also known as the Plane of Assiah. In later chapters, we will work through the other three levels, moving in order from the mental, up to the creative and finally to the penthouse of the metaphysical energies, the archetypa, the Plane of Ideas, where you'll meet the cosmic forces of the Archangels.

Remember, we mentioned before that four is also an important number? You've seen above how it has teamed up with the number seven at times, but four also stands alone for important features.

Four is most often familiar in the term "four-square" and in the ancient alchemist's lexicon it's the number of the earth. Earth itself is the fourth planet from the Sun, while we talk of things being dispersed to the four corners of the Universe. Earth is bounded by the four cardinal points of north, south, east and west, while the four Archangels rule at the four points of the compass: Uriel to the north, Michael to the south, Raphael to the east and Gabriel to the west.

Regardless of the Scientific Table of Elements - they came much later - the four alchemical elements are Earth, Air, Fire and Water, matching with the four qualities of Hot, Cold, Wet and Dry. The elements are the first stage in the growth and development of first matter (our earth), and each of the elements combine two of the four qualities. For instance, Fire is hot and dry; Earth is dry and cold and so on. And these qualities and elements we cannot do without. They keep us alive. The duties of some of the Angels is to look after these and keep them in balance. They (the Angels) control nature and the stars and are also in charge of human affairs. We feel sorry for the Angels of Air when we see the pollution they have to clean up, just to keep materialistic mortals in reasonably good shape. So it is with the other Angels who look after the rest of the elements and qualities. No wonder they also get sick at times (i.e. drained of energy) and further on in the book you will learn how to help them recover with the use of your own directed energy.

According to metaphysical wisdom, at the beginning of our spiritual climb, there are four Worlds we work through. These Worlds are often referred to as "levels". It is easier to understand that term as we move upwards through the levels of our own minds. These levels are divisions between the Nothingness and our own material world. In this continuous process of working back towards the Divinity, our inner minds encounter each level, meeting these different Angel energies with whom we form relationships for different purposes. On the second level, you'll encounter the Angels of the Astral Light who help the seeker across the Mind Walk to meet another part of the Inner Self. Third level Angels help to flood the Chakras with light as they are opened. And at the fourth level you meet the really bright lights of Angels at your major initiation when you open the Mystic Door.

Angels, you will realize are concerned with form (formulation). Therefore, we have to learn to activate the forces of the Universe to get the Angels to manipulate this force to bring it towards us in the form we have requested. It doesn't matter which level you are working on, you'll have to apply this same strategy to achieve either spiritual or material results.

The top level, number four, is called the Archetypal where all ideas originate - call it the drawing office if you like. Ideas of how the human race (humanity) can benefit and develop have been handed down in the shape of fire, the wheel, numbers, machinery, computers, the written word, story ideas (including this book). Even war machines and things we consider horrifying have their start here, although the purposes they were put to by devious human minds did not originate here.

Take the airplane for instance. A marvelous invention used to move the mail quickly from one place to another, now to move food from one country to another where a particular product cannot be grown. Now consider wartime where they are used with the intent to destroy.

There are two sides to everything and anything can be used either way by people. The automobile is another example of a brilliant invention making use of the world's resources, oil and gasoline, (courtesy of the Angels) which gets us from one place to another swiftly, instead of spending days and nights on the road with a horse and cart. But cars also kill. So do many other things which have been manufactured, but when they are used wisely they benefit everybody. Get the idea?

In the following chapter, you will be able to investigate the two sides of your own energy patterns and decide how constructive and/or destructive they are to your life.

Now, on to the next level, number three, which is called the Creative plane. Where those ideas from the Archetypal level are worked on and tested until they are perfected, and in a sufficient state for the innovative and inventive minds of humans to reach out for. And if the Angels find they don't work out as they were expected to, they get thrown out or put aside to be worked on at a future time; perhaps even centuries ahead when other generations are ready for them.

One that got away that you might be amused at happened way back in 1916 when a slightly retarded Angel (and yes, there are some) whispered to an inventor that he could make ice without water. The idea, which was quietly snuck by the testing Angels, was that you could go ice-skating in summer on an artificial rink that consisted of soluble glass, fluor-calcium, asbestos, ground glass, paraffin and soapstone. Naturally, it didn't work and finally somebody else found it would be easier to manufacture real ice. That worked, and the artificial stuff went into the astral garbage pail.

But like we said, sometimes it takes a while for ideas to catch on. The zipper, for instance, originally called the slide fastener, was floated onto the mental scene before 1892 when a patent was granted for that new-fangled idea! Yet it wasn't until 1917 that a

17

wily designer noticed it would only take a tiny improvement in the shape of the teeth to make the zipper practical so that it could be mass produced. Twenty five years after the thought was passed on from the Creative plane, it came into being.

And how about the fax machine having to wait around. The idea was on the ether in the 1800's and in 1863 author Jules Verne included it in his novel "Paris in the Twentieth Century". The setting of the novel was the 1960's. It was rejected by his publisher who felt his readers would not accept it. It was too far fetched and nobody would believe his prophecies. Verne never submitted his manuscript to any other publisher, but hid it away in a safe.

Just over a hundred years later the idea was picked up by another creative mind and put into practical use with the public in mind, and the facsimile (fax) machine became common place. And in 1989 Jules Verne's novel was discovered in the safe, which was thought to be empty, and this deserving work was finally published in France in 1994 and in England in 1996.

You've all heard the winter noises of snow toys. Roughly eighty years ago Bombardier tuned into an idea and put a car engine on a sled. For those who love them, that's how the original snowmobile was born.

In 1913, an Englishman named Harry Brearley tuned into the idea of an alloy which he developed into stainless steel, and very usefully became the cutlery with which you eat your food.

These are just a few things that have happened. New developments are happening so fast and furious in our world of reality, and we wonder if our minds are becoming more spiritually attuned so that we can touch these ideas more easily? Certainly there is a much greater movement nowadays towards spiritual development and understanding. But on the other hand there are a tremendous number of deaths taking place, and some very brilliant minds have gone on to the Other Side. They are continuing on with the work they would have carried out here, contributing their expertise towards new developments for the progress of our earth and humanity. Many of them are also helping with the balancing of world karma.

What a wonderful place this Creative plane is. Meditation (which you shall learn later on) is called for to touch these marvelous energy patterns which are floating within this world. Once the mind is in this meditative state, it can bring back those ideas which are transferred into the next lower level. This one, number two, is called the Mental plane which is available to all minds. These ideas can be formulated into something more concrete in nature which then appear on the material plane, number one, as something that can be used here in this world. Remember how an idea suddenly pops into your mind, especially if you're day-dreaming? You've mentally tuned into this pool of knowledge which you probably find useful and beneficial.

Apart from these four planes where all things seem to exist, what else is number 4? Well, if you add these two important numbers 7 and 4, you get 11, a power number. Now multiply 11 by 2 and you get another power number, 22. That number represents the 22 paths of the Cabala, the Tree of Life, the knowledge of the Inner Worlds, which was given to the Chosen Ones (Initiates) by courtesy of the Angels. It was handed down to them from the Archetypal level where all ideas are born, then sent down to the Creative level where it was perfected further, then to the Mental level where the minds of the Initiates could pick it up. They developed it into picture form for use on the physical plane of matter as a mental ladder to climb back towards the Divinity - the Oneness, Zero, rather like the serpent with its tail in its mouth.

These 22 paths represent the two sides of everything from spiritual to material - up and down; black and white; coming and going; positive and negative; the dark and light side of yourself; the one and the many; the limited and unlimited; man and woman; square and oblong; straight and curved; motion and rest; as above, so below ....the list is purposely endless. Part of which we will cover in another chapter and the balance in the two final chapters, along with the four axioms of the spiritual world which are Know, Will, Dare and Keep Silent.

By now, you must be getting the idea that numbers are important. Indeed they are. The Universe is based on numbers; they are the clues to the real, underlying structure of the Universe. First, it was null and void, then the intelligences appeared by reason of the four elements. Later, as the gods were formed, they named these intelligences "Angels" and the structure began to change as the gods realized they could use these Angel energies for different purposes.

Now, recognize that once something has been named it develops a reality of its own and can be manipulated for good or for its opposite, namely bad. And if the gods hadn't given names to the intelligences you wouldn't have a group of Guardian Angels (whose names you now know) and other Angels on different higher up levels whom you can influence to help you through life. If you re-read and absorb this chapter you will discern the connections between each paragraph which will now lead you into the next chapter to discover the consequences of these associations.

Chapter 3
Setting Up your Personal Relationship

ow that you know the names of your Angels, you can begin a personal relationship with them. All these years they have been waiting for this contact, and they will be very pleased and responsive towards your reaching out. How do you do this? In your mind, for a start.

First of all, take time out for a quiet sit somewhere. Make it your own private place at the same time each day; thereby setting up a regular pattern which your mind can recognize and look forward to. Settle down and relax as much as possible, then let your mind roam free for a while. Now think on the names of your Angels, but don't expect immediate response or you will end up being disappointed, telling yourself, "It doesn't work". Just have faith and the contact will eventually happen. You have to build up the rapport first just as you do when you make a new friendship on this physical plane.

Once you are comfortable with thinking about your Angels (and this may take a few quiet sitting times), visualize how you would like them to look (sans wings of course, the church stuck those on!). This visualization is the important part of the start of your association with your new friends. You have to begin with mind pictures. Remember, Angels are just energy patterns, they have no faces, features or physical bodies, and you have to create a mental link - a body of light to start up the connection. So you are at liberty to view them however you wish, and these thought forms are purely your creation. You may picture just one or the whole group together, although one is easier for a start. So let's start

21

with one.

Consider this single one to be a portrait you are painting. Think of the coloring of the skin, the hair, the eyes, the eyebrows, the shape of the features, the facial expression. Is it kind or stern? Smiling or whimsical? Is this energy pattern tall, short, thin, plump, broad shouldered, or wiry and muscled? Is your Angel old and wise, full of knowledge to share, the comforting type? Or is he/she young and sprightly raring to share experiences with you? What's your choice? Whatever you have decided, hold a firm picture in your mind.

Now consider the clothing you are going to paint onto your portrait. Does he/she wear a long gown, carry a staff, wear earrings as the old and wise did in a long era past? Have you chosen modern day clothes, a pant suit, jeans and T-shirt, sweat shirt or something in between? Search the encyclopedia of your mind for the most comfortable fit for your mental portrait. Finally, you need to select the colors of the garments, then mentally stand back and ask yourself if you are satisfied with your portrait. Is it what you want? Does it make you feel happy to look at it? Consider and study your emotions as you view your handiwork. Does it fill you with joy and feelings of elation? Would you like a relationship with what you have created? You would? Good. You're off to an excellent start. If not, repaint your portrait.

Now, pick a frame for it as if you were going to hang it on your living room wall. Once you have framed it, hang it on your mental wall and send warm loving thoughts to this painted visualization. You will be surprised at what will take place as this rapport grows in strength.

At this point, some of you may consider that this seems like a silly thing to do, making mental pictures, but just recall how you think and feel when you've just met and fallen in love with someone. Think of how you picture scenes in your mind of him/her, the growth and closeness getting stronger, the love developing and blossoming. As these mental scenes take place in your mind, so your loving energy patterns are received and experienced by your boy/girl friend. Then they are returned to you in equal measure and expansion. So it is with developing the Angel energies – the same thing happens when you use visualization and mental pictures.

When you feel this relationship has taken root, and you will know within yourself that something is happening, you can do the same thing to activate the energy patterns of your whole group. This just takes a little more work.

For instance, think of being all together on an outing or a picnic. Where will you place your group? On the beach? In a park at a picnic setting? A mountain scene? In a quiet country glade absorbing the sun's rays? On a river bank surrounded by trees? Whatever scene you choose, visualize every detail of the surrounding and of each Angel: height, coloring, clothing and so on, just as you did before when you created your single portrait.

Visualize the setting until it is strong and firm in your mind, then put your people in their places and get your mental camera ready. When you feel sure that everything is firmly embedded in your mind, take your picture, then put it in your mental photograph album. Send your thoughts of love and enjoyment to this group picture, and, as with your single portrait, any time you wish to make contact, bring the mental pictures to the forefront of your mind and your people will be there.

Remember, all this work is done within your mind, each day, in the quiet place you have selected for yourself. This is the beginning of your mind training, which, in the months and years to come will lead you into some of the most fabulous experiences you will ever have.

Now, within your mind, it's time to open up a dialogue with your Angels. Think what you would like to say, how you will open up this communication. Once this has taken place and you have enjoyed your talk, remember to thank your people for their love, concern and energy and know within yourself that all will be well. Then close down your mental channel.

You do this by gradually opening your eyes, and letting the room come into focus. Feel the chair you are sitting on beneath you and become aware of where you are. Slowly re-orient yourself back into the mundane every day world, close off your thoughts of your Angels and become part of your physical existence again.

"Why do I need to do this visualizing?" you ask. Apart from the fact that you need to create thought forms as we described earlier, (which you do unconsciously all day, every day) your mind needs an anchor of some description, a focal point if you wish. Otherwise, it will go off in all directions thinking about everything and nothing worthwhile, groping in the dark, so to speak. This is your Inner Mind you are dealing with (your subconscious mind) over which *you* must take control.

Now, this Inner Mind has always been in control of you, sending up thoughts of all sorts to your conscious mind to which you respond without thinking about them or considering the consequences of that thought or action. That mind has always been the master, but if you wish to achieve both your material and your spiritual needs *you* have to become the master. Not an easy task by any means. Your Inner Mind will find all sorts of ways to detract you from taking over. After all, it's been the boss all your life, so why should it give up its position now? Ignore its moaning, whining and deviousness and persevere.

So first, the strong building of the portrait and the album picture, gradually getting control over your Inner Mind. Once this is achieved, you can really start your conversation. Ah yes, but what to say?

Now, let's think about that for a moment. If you had just been introduced to a new person or group of people, how would you handle this situation? Remember, each of you will react differently when you meet new people, so you'll just have to wing this one as just the person you are. Here are a few suggestions to get you started.

How about describing your day to your Angels. Tell about the things you've done, the people you've talked to, what you accomplished, something you are especially interested in, the things you intend to do tomorrow, next week or whenever. The sort of things you'd talk about with your new friend(s) as you gradually get a rapport going. Think back on how you've built up an intimacy with people and apply this same technique to your Angel people. Believe us, these intelligences will absorb the energy patterns of your thought conversation, and yes, they *will* be interested in what you do, how you think and how you approach your life in this material world. After all, they have been responsible for you since your birth, and they would like to hear how you are responding to their guidance.

As you are gradually intertwined into their energies, you will begin to pick up tendrils of mental responses – their answers in fact.

So how do you know they are talking to you, and you are not talking to yourself? You don't really, not at first. In fact, for quite a while you *will* be talking to yourself until your energy patterns and the Angels energies create a mental telephone line between you. Keep on going, don't give up, because one day things will feel mentally different. You'll feel a knowingness, a lightness, almost an airiness, a kind of wispiness; perhaps even a feeling of warmth steal over you. You will know with a certainty which we cannot describe. There are no words to encompass this feeling that somebody is there and the communication is starting and valid. Listen, interpret what you think you hear, and try to keep logic out (it will creep in for sure, Inner Mind does not want to give up its position), because what you hear may well be able to prove itself somehow in your day to day living, which will give you more confidence in your Angel connections.

Getting away from your Angels for a short while, we need to discuss positive thinking, because this is the basis of your success on all levels of the Path. Whether it's physical, mental or completely spiritual work, positive thinking works miracles. Let's begin with the majority of people's basic requirements, the physical need for money. First, let us clear up a fundamental misconception. We've spoken to many disappointed people about positive thinking and their message has been almost the same, "It doesn't work. I've read *all* the books and I've tried all the methods. I've hoped for money. I've willed that money shall come my way. I've asked for money. I've wanted money with all my heart and soul, and I'm still poor. Positive thinking doesn't work."

Now, let's take that apart phrase by phrase.

First, the sentence "It doesn't work." This is a negative for a start. Doesn't, Does NOT - is a negative phrase - a denying phrase. And, for the people who say it, it proves that positive thinking *does* work – even if, in this case, it achieves a negative result. They have made a very positive statement of fact: it doesn't work and sure enough, it doesn't. Proving to itself that any statement made with a firm belief behind it, comes true. So if *you* believe that this communication with your Angels doesn't work, you can be sure it won't. Isn't it odd that we find it so much easier to be negative than we do to be positive?

You know, it only takes a slight twitch of the brain to reach the conclusion that if you change the words a little and say, "It *does* work", then it *will* work. And it happens to be true, but only if *you* happen to believe it to be true, and you've seen it in action.

Let's take the next bit of the "doesn't work" thought. "I've read all the books." Fine, reading broadens the mind, it broadens the backside, too. And unless you become selective in your reading habits, it can mix you up and slow you down; trying this method and then the next and so on. But if you really look at all the books on positive thinking, they'll all tell you to visualize the end result as if it is already true.

And the next phrase? "I've hoped for money." Fine, for years kids have been hoping it won't rain tomorrow – and dashed hopes have washed out more picnics than you can shake a stick at. "I've willed for money," etc. Willpower is great – but visualization nearly always overcomes will power in the long run. "I've asked for money." Ask and it shall be given – if you know who to ask! "I've wanted money." Now that's a negative word if you like. To want something is to be short of it. To want money means you are short of it and in the name of positive thinking, if you announce that you want money, you're very likely to go on wanting.

"And I'm still poor." And you're likely to stay that way until you can say, and believe "I'm rich."

Maxwell Maltz in his book Psycho Cybernetics approaches the idea of positive thinking in a unique way. He suggests that you are the driver of a machine. The machine is you and if you strive towards a goal, whatever that goal is, the machine that is you will move towards it successfully. So if your own self-image sees you as a failure, you'll become a failure, (a back to front success), if it sees you as a success you'll become a success. And if your self thinks of you as mediocre, that's what you will be. Same with poor, rich, sick, well – set a goal for the machine (self) and it will work towards it.

And your machine learns to function successfully by experiencing success. The interesting thing is that your machine, nervous system, your goal seeking mechanism, call it what you will, cannot tell the difference between an actual experience and an experience imagined vividly in detail. So two important factors here are: setting clear goals and seeing the goals accomplished. And later, when you are meditating regularly, spend a few minutes seeing yourself successful. If it's clothes you need, see yourself out for a stroll in whatever you want to wear. If it's bills that need paying, visualize yourself **receiving the receipted bill**. Notice this: see the bill already paid - let your subconscious work on the steps of how to do it. And don't let anyone say that using your visualizing power for material things for yourself is wrong. The physical plane is just as holy as the seventh plane. Divinity made them all, and material things are just as right as spiritual things. It's the balance that counts – enough material to balance the spiritual.

Visualizing most definitely works. Way back in the 60's when we were teaching metaphysics, we decided to have get-togethers on Saturday evenings and found there were not enough little tables to go round. Coffee cups were being put on the floor and spilt and it was inconvenient, so we started visualizing. It took three days. A lady who lived a few doors down, to whom we had only spoken casually, asked us if we could make use of a coffee table. She was moving into an apartment at the end of the month and didn't have room for it. It was also brand new, she had bought it, stuck it under her bed still in its original carton and forgotten she had it! We still have that table.

28

Another time it worked for us when we needed some ephemerides for our astrology classes. None of the bookshops carried them, so we went into visualizing action. A short time later we were browsing in the local book store when the manager told us he had received a box of second hand books and there was "some astrology stuff" in the bottom. Did we want it? So visualization – positive thinking works and we still use the same system for ourselves when we have a need for material things. Now, does it work for spiritual things?

Believe that it does. See yourself progressing spiritually, set a clear goal and you will meet that goal.

It's the goal setting that's the challenge. Material things are easy to visualize, but how do you visualize an abstract concept? How do you see yourself as spiritually mature, nearer to the Divine Power? Answer: thoughts need to be as pure as the driven snow. How? We've covered the first bit discussing negative thinking patterns, and the second is removing anger, resentment and corrosive thoughts.

Anger and resentment you can see in yourself quite easily. In fact, if you were clairvoyant, you would see anger in other people as rather nasty oozing black pools and puddles within their aura. Your own aura would look the same. Resentment is actually harmful to your physical, mental and emotional health. So consider this: you know when you're mad at someone. You know when someone or some thing has annoyed you. Now, we have to recognize another basic. Your anger, resentment or annoyance is nothing at all to do with the other person or the thing which is bugging you. It's your reaction to the situation which causes the annoyance or anger and eventually, somewhere, sometime, you'll come to realize that *you're* the problem, not them or it. And what do you accomplish by getting angry, feeling resentment towards others or continuing to think corrosive thoughts about someone

29

else? All you are doing is gnawing away at your own peace of mind and blocking the next step on the ladder of Light. Relax. Relax and think of it this way. If you were deaf, you would not hear what others were saying and you would not react. And if you were blind, you also would not react to the facial expressions of others, for you would not see them.

Let's take this one step further and look at speech patterns which can also be harmful to yourself - and conversely - rewarding by altering them. Do you think of what you are going to say before you open your mouth? Probably not, untrained minds rarely do - but try this one on for size. When you are with a group of people, listen very carefully to what they say. Do you hear comments like "Joe gives me a pain in the neck", I can't get through to them, it's like banging my head against a brick wall", "My mother-in-law is a pain in the rear end", "So and so gets under my skin," "It burns me up," "Makes me sick," "Sick of this job." Do you find yourself using these same speech patterns? When these utterances are made with real force behind them, it's not surprising that people are sick. People make themselves sick. That thought put into words comes winging back just like a boomerang.

"Pain in the neck," full of tension in the neck and shoulders which affects sleeping patterns, never feeling fully rested, leading to irritation and short temper. See the connection, the consequence, which, of course is cause and effect? "Banging my head against a brick wall" - oh those headaches or migraines at just the *thought* of it. "Pain in the rear end," those hemorrhoids really are painful and makes sitting down a further problem. "Gets under my skin," what are all those little pimples, eruptions and raised bumps on your skin? "Makes me sick" "Sick of this job" – feeling bad in your stomach, are you? Always a little bit uncomfortable or fractionally nauseated, taking more time off from work because you don't feel well? "It burns me up," got a nasty attack of heartburn? We're sure you've got the idea by now and hopefully got the message.

So how about putting these concepts into practice right now? For three days try positive thinking all day, watch your speech patterns, and try not to react to whatever is going on in your environment. Remember the three wise monkeys: hear no evil, see no evil and speak no evil. It is a good start, and if you can manage to do three days without faltering, continue on day by day until it becomes a habit. It's an interesting challenge, and challenge is what you'll frequently meet as you travel the Path. What you are practicing is the art of causing changes in consciousness which bring changes into your life. And you are encouraging your own mental powers and inherent physical capabilities to become more acute.

So let's briefly review those steps.

Number 1. Belief. It comes with practice in believing. Doubts and fears are the enemies of belief. Next time you find a doubt in your own abilities creeping up on you, take the thought out into the light of your mind and tell it to "GO", very positively. After a while, you'll find it works – like a charm. For it is, if you like, a sort of spell. Once you get the belief going, it grows. It's the success making success all over again.

Number 2. Relax. That should be coming easier now. You've been doing it for a while, and provided you have been practicing regularly, you should see some improvement in yourself and your environment.

Number 3. Tune in. Relax in the quiet and move into the silence. What are you tuning into? Your Angels who surround you, who are part of the Divine Power, and also into your inner self as we shall see in the next chapter.

Number 4. Acceptance. Around about the time when tuning-in becomes a reality for you, you will also find intuition - hunches if you like - gradually becoming stronger. Look for new ideas too. Ask yourself if what you are receiving will give you more serenity or satisfaction. If the answer is "yes", then you know that your intuition is good. You may even find that you have a hunch - a precognition - a knowing of the future. Perhaps it's a solution to someone else's problem, or even a solution to a problem that you didn't know existed. This is perfectly natural because you are now honing your inner powers.

Number 5. Visualize. Follow your hunches and act on them. Visualize and get. Here we step firmly into the world of cause and effect. Plant a firm visualization, and sooner or later it is going to materialize. So assist your visualization by obeying your intuitions as soon as they appear. Intuitions and visualizations go hand-in-hand to achieve your desires. Believe you have what you want and act as if you've already got it. Stop hoping and wishing and ACT. Polish up your belief. Move in hard on canceling out negativity, anger and reactions to petty irritations. And watch your mouth, think before you speak. What will be the consequences of what you say?

Number 6. Expand. You can do this by taking a look at yourself: who you are, what you have been and what you are going to become in the future. So let's find out in the next chapter.

Chapter 4
Making a Profile of Yourself

Our Angels are here to help you make your life better. They helped shepherd you into this world and they have a major interest in your welfare. Any time you consult with them, they will help you make changes and to see things from a different perspective. If you would like to receive their help, now is the time to put together a profile of yourself.

Why a profile? Well, first of all, getting to know the real you is a wonderful experience. This is not the persona you think you know that you show to the outside world. That's just the mask you wear. The true hidden self is a shining light.

Secondly, to reach your true hidden self, you'll have to get rid of the baggage you're carrying which has been dumped on you by the outside world from the moment you were able to understand words and commands. You are not alone. The majority of us got the same treatment during our growing up years because we trusted everybody around us. And within that trust, we were molded into what we have become, not what we truly want to be.

Now it's time to break the mold. Your inner self knows what you've chosen to experience and achieve in this incarnation – and so do your Angels. They'll stand on guard to guide you towards whatever it is you choose to become.

Question: What do you want to be, what do you want to become? What do you want to achieve? Everything is possible when you shuck off the past, and move into the present from which you can control your future.

Now, write down how you would like your life to be. Norman Vincent Peale said, "We tend to get what we expect." And Henry Ford said, "Whether you think you can or can't - you're right." Remember those statements as you work to change your life.

Be honest with yourself. Write down your fears, obsessions, fixations and any negative approaches you have to certain aspects of your life. The really negative ones are the strong demons of self which disturb you, then get pushed into the background, remaining unrecognized, because you are too fearful to face them. You then continue to carry them around like an old useless sack. If those images have the power to disturb you to that extent, wouldn't it make sense to face them with that same power, and make the change to positive growth?

Take a good look at your values, beliefs and prejudices. Recognize that learned habits, attitudes and expectations affect the way you think. Become aware of them, change them if they are not useful to you. And also recognize that thoughts are things (thought forms which we've mentioned before) which become reality; because the awesome power of the mind can become either a destructive or constructive weapon.

So who are you? What are your beliefs? Remember these are the opinions or the points of view that you have developed over a period of time, as a result of what you have learned and experienced. Are they really your own true beliefs? Recall those first seven years of your life and what you learned from parents and family members? These are the beliefs that affect how you behave now, and they can hold you back or propel you forward.

Think about that, then take yourself back into your past and see for yourself what has taken place for you to become as you are.

34

You will then recognize what is holding you back from experiencing a happy and useful life.

So here comes the difficult, and for some people, the painful bit of confronting the worst of oneself, the demons which torture our souls. An exercise book like the kids use at school is a very useful adjunct. Skip the first page and use the double page which comes up next. Draw a line down the center of each page. Now you will have four wide columns, two on each page. Put these headings on the top of each column, and your pages should look something like this.

Beliefs	What or Why	Antidotes	Changes
Fear of	strange places	self-reliance	
	men/women	boldness	
	heights	courage	
Hatred of	self	self respect	
	father/mother	understanding	
	teacher	acceptance	
	authority	cooperation	
Anger towards	world	change outlook	
	partner		
	child		
Resentment of	co-worker	generosity	
Shame	humiliation	strength to face issues	
Guilt	quick temper	control thought	
Lack of	confidence	self esteem	
Unworthiness		self-assurance	

We've filled in a few suggestions to give you an idea of how to fill in your columns. You will have other things you wish to put in as there are innumerable hang-ups to choose from, and each person's will be different and so will the solution. Changes that you make will be added to that column at a later date when they take place.

Write down all your fears, one underneath each other on the left hand side of the page. Then write down where they came from, if you can remember. If you can't, don't worry, memory might bring it back later. It may not be your fear but one transmitted to you by a parent, relative, neighbor or close friend during your very young period when others had control over your development. Recognize that fears are demons from the unconscious which produce doubts, and doubts need to be vanquished by self confidence.

Next, ask yourself if you have anger. This is a major transgression against your outer self, your inner self, your soul. It's a violation of a healthy body. This offence produces sickness of all sorts, for it is, in itself, a cancer which is eating away at you. Write it down in the left hand column, the why of it on the right hand side, against whom or what. Most of us have some sort of anger at some time or another, but if yours is permanent and directed against the world in general, then you have a major problem, because you've created it with your own attitude towards the world. Really, the world has done nothing to you. As we said in the previous chapter, it's your reaction to events surrounding you that makes you feel the world hates you and you respond in anger, which eventually becomes a vicious circle.

Other things to consider: Do you feel humiliation, apprehension, fear of the future, greed, jealousy, unworthiness? Do you lack ambition? Are you a worry pot? Then search for the cause. Are you judging and condemning yourself because you feel you are a failure? Did you know that fear of failure is because you fear someone else's disapproval or ridicule? You don't need any of this garbage, it only leads you into unhappiness.

Get all these things down on the left hand side of your page, then you'll be able to recognize yourself and what is happening to you. If all these questions are answered honestly, a clear view of the path ahead will start to open up before you. Especially when you get to writing down all your good points which will bring the balance.

Recall in the first chapter those seven year cycles we mentioned? Tie these in with your learned responses and recall the control other people had over you. Do people still have control over you through your emotions? Do you allow this to happen because you want them to think well of you, so that you are constantly trying to please all the people all of the time? Understand that by doing this, people will take advantage of you, which can create a feeling of dissatisfaction within yourself. You are not being true to yourself. Look at your emotions. If they control you, use your awareness to take charge. Learned responses are the equivalent of self destructiveness resulting in a lack of responsibility for yourself.

Now, if all this self destructive behavior is holding you back from living the life of happiness, which is really your due, then these obsessions and negativities must be eliminated and replaced by healthy thinking. You didn't choose all these things when you decided to reincarnate. Much of this suffering arises from your own reaction to the experiences – not the experiences themselves, which we need for growth and understanding. It's the lack of controlled reaction that brings you pain. So recognize it for what it is. You've gone through it, you've paid that bit of Karmic debt, so let it go. Instead, work on mental purification which will bring you real peace of mind, and you'll find that self discovery really and truly is an exciting experience.

Getting back to your notebook, you can fill in the other two columns on the right hand page as you discover the antidote to your problems, and experience the changes which are taking place within you. Yes, indeed, you will most certainly change as you recognize the futility of your problems and decide on a new life for yourself.

This reminds us of a student we had in one of our classes who was mourning the loss of her sister who had drowned. She was absolutely inconsolable, and we'd tried everything we could think of to make her see that nothing could erase what had happened. The past was gone and she had to put it behind her and get on with her life. A chance remark (which we've now forgotten) made us ask when this accident had taken place. To our consternation she confessed that her sister had drowned a couple of years before she was born, and her mother had told her that if her sister had lived she wouldn't be here now. This young girl had lived with this guilt (not of her own making, but perpetuated by herself) for all these years, knowing she was only a replacement who didn't match up to what her sister was going to be (according to her mother). Now that we had all the facts, we had a handle on the situation and could start to deal with it.

First of all, we drew up the columns for her as we have suggested for you in the previous pages. She had a *fear* of drowning implanted by her mother which held her back from enjoying swimming, boating or any other activities which involved being on or near the water. She had never been allowed these activities and did not recognize that this fear was not her own. She constantly refused invitations from friends who enjoyed them. They eventually left her alone, not being able to understand her hang-up, which she herself didn't really understand.

Guilt came up next. If her sister had lived, she wouldn't be here. Therefore, she felt she really had no place in being a member of the household. She also felt *unworthy* because she was a replacement, not the original. And in her mind she was at fault. Can you see what a lousy bed-mate guilt is? It takes up so much of the mental bed leaving a feeling of unrest.

First off, we had to get her to fully understand that the guilt she felt was not hers. It was her mother who actually felt guilty and irresponsible for allowing her child to play unattended near an unfenced swimming pool. Her mother was able to push these feelings into the background when Amy was born using her as a scapegoat, but calling it protection. Amy's feelings of unworthiness were unconsciously implanted by herself when she was told her mother only intended to have one child. Somehow, Amy believed she was responsible for her sister's death, but she was unable to express how she felt – her *shame* (next item) was too strong to be revealed.

We could see changes happening as Amy thought through her life, and then realization dawned that she was being used as a pawn. Now she could see that her life was not real. *Hatred* of her mother took the place of guilt and she felt *contempt* for her father and saw him as a weak person overshadowed by her mother. Having worked through her previous feelings about herself, hatred and contempt took over - a natural response - and she had to deal with these. Strength, courage, determination and a certain amount of self esteem were developing in Amy. Finally, she could see and understand her parents humiliation, their own shame and guilt (remember the two sides of everything?). And eventually she was able to forgive them, forgive herself for her previous beliefs and give herself permission to get rid of these beliefs. A huge step in the right direction for Amy. With our help and the guidance from her Angels, she was no longer a non-entity. What a mental purification! She had an identity of her own. She was at last her own person developing inner strength and skills, choosing the things that were most important to her.

With mind over matter and a different perspective and personality, she was able to define her vision, discovering ways to develop it and, to her delight, she attracted to herself the resources needed to let her vision grow.

She had a lot of other things to work through, and it took many months of courage and hard work on her part to get her life under her own control. Further changes gradually took place as mind and body made the connection bringing about belief in herself which led to self healing and a new life.

You can do the same thing for yourself. Look at the antidote of the negative qualities you have written in your journal. Do you already have some of these positive qualities lying deep within you, which you have not recognized or even realized you have? Perhaps they are simply overlaid by the sea of negativity in which you swim.

Again, you need to investigate yourself. This time in a lighter vein. Sit back and think about yourself, then write down all the good qualities you think you possess. Don't stint yourself or start to become modest about your attributes; they are likely to lift you over and above the previous life you have been living. You'll be able to recognize your worth, and as your changes take place you'll recognize your values and put them into positive action.

Thinking back on people we've met, there was a realtor we would have liked to help, but as she had not asked for it we could not interfere. There is an occult law that says we shall not interfere with another person's life unless they specifically ask for help, as they may be working through part of their karma. Anyway, we were in another province which we visited every two months to do T.V., radio, readings, lectures, and seminars. We were always busy, often staying over longer than we wanted. We decided it might be worthwhile to purchase a small property rather than paying out for the penthouse suite which we rented on each visit. We found a few interesting properties in the newspaper, called the realtor and she eventually came over to see us. She came through the door rather reluctantly, refused a comfortable chair and sat on the floor, but she wouldn't raise her head to look at us. We wondered where this interview would take us. Finally, she confessed that when we told her over the phone to take the elevator up to the penthouse suite she tried to find another realtor to see us, as she thought she wasn't good enough to help us. Now there's unworthiness for you. All because of a penthouse suite and what she thought we would think of her! Would she have felt the same, we wondered, if we had been staying in an ordinary room? This was a totally self-made reaction, as are other negative opinions. In fact, being absorbed with one's self: self-consciousness, judging self, criticizing self is sheer destruction of a healthy mind and body. Naturally, she didn't find us a property, didn't even take us to see what we had picked out. She said she was "afraid" we might not like what she had to offer, even though we had picked out what we would like to view.

Here was fear creeping into the picture as well. It had control over her behavior which limited her motivation, potential and her creative expression. It also had a direct influence on her relationship with us, and we could see the jagged colors in her aura that her fear had created. We probed a little, quite gently, but we could see we would not get very far. She couldn't bring herself to express her fear of life and her feelings of unworthiness even though she was aware of the work we did in helping people. Unfortunately, she was unable to help herself right then by speaking up to ask for help. We sometimes wonder if she was able to make life changes, but we never saw her again.

41

Do you recall that at the end of chapter 2 we mentioned that giving a name to something gives it power and identity? Go back to your journal for a moment and review what you have written about yourself. Now think about these things you have named and note how they have control over you. You have allowed the demons from your unconscious mind to produce these fears, obsessions and whatever else you have written in your journal. Right now, they are the masters and you must instigate change to put them in the background and take control of your own life. You will find it much easier to deal with a problem, a fear or whatever since you have put a name to it, because now it becomes recognition and you can have control, instead of IT controlling you. This may not make the problem go away immediately, but at least you will know what you are dealing with. By naming the antidote, you change the power from negative to positive and you also change the destiny/karma of that energy pattern. Study the debit and credit sheet of your personal assets and this will aid you in your decision making.

Let's have a look at names in a different direction. What is your own name? Do you like it? As a matter of fact, you chose your name before you reincarnated. The vibrations of that name being important to your soul growth at that time. This was impressed on the subconscious mind of your parents and they carried out the plan, thereby placing you under their control. If you really dislike your name, you may find it is inhibiting your growth and change, as your folks may still have control over you one way or another. Your soul is also discreetly pointing out that you have completed and overcome that particular karmic vibration.

Have fun with yourself. Change your name if you don't like the one you have. Names are potent. Even though they are only labels they reflect some of the aspect of the face you turn to the world. So by changing the one you have, you will change your personality into something new. This new way of thinking will make you happier than the old way. And by taking this step you will also change your karmic pattern.

Reinvent yourself for what you would like your life to be or even reinvent your past if you don't like what you had. If you tell yourself often enough that this was the way it was instead of what you experienced, you'll eventually come to believe it, and what happened previously will no longer exist. Once you do it and really believe it, you'll find the world is different, and bit by bit you'll have less baggage to carry around. There is nothing to stop you from reinventing the world to suit yourself. As a matter of fact, if you don't change your bit of the world, the world is likely to change yours to suit itself. If you find this suggestion to be a bit of a challenge, an easy way to do it is to pretend you are a writer, story-teller, or play-write. Make up or imagine a story of a life you would like, add all the characters and use yourself as the central character. Then add a satisfactory ending that you can bask in. This will most definitely do the trick. So discover and explore all your options, put them into action and enjoy your brand new life.

Looking back at our example list again and noting "fear of strange places", this frequently involves a fear of death which rarely gets brought out into the open, and this seems to be a good place to discuss it. The older one gets, the more it seems to weigh heavily for some people. Especially in moments of loneliness or sadness, knowing there is nothing to be done to stop this approaching event. It is inevitable when we reach the end of our physical career – our physical life when the body no longer can or will fulfill its functions. But we can prepare in advance a road map for ourselves of that journey when physical death closes the door on this mundane existence.

As a matter of fact, when you go to sleep each night, in effect, you are "dying", having become mentally detached from the

43

physical world. Your soul pops off into the Inner Planes and enjoys itself, but it is still attached by the silver cord that we mentioned earlier. It then comes back, refreshed, into your physical body ready for the next day. Now that isn't in the least bit painful, is it? In fact, if you can remember your dreams, your sensations, feelings, the people you meet, the happiness and joy your soul receives on its nightly visit, you would never experience fear of death again.

When you sleep, you gradually move into different levels of consciousness, which you call your dream world, and when you die you take this consciousness with you. It continues on in the Planes, taking with it all you have learned and absorbed here on the earth plane. Now, wouldn't it be rather nice to know in advance which place you are going to when you've finished with your physical body? Of course it would. If you were going on a journey somewhere, you would consult a road map and pick your route before you started out, wouldn't you? You can do the same thing now by investigating the Inner Planes Paths and absorbing this information into your consciousness and you will know exactly where you will end up. So let's look at how to draw this so-called road map. Very simply, it entails relaxation and stilling of the physical body (just as you do in sleep), then proceeding into meditation (see chapter 6) and keeping your awareness focused within. The major objective of this exercise is that wherever you may go in your conscious mind and whatever happens to your awareness (which you call "I"), at a deeper level there is a communion between your inner mind, a portion of your soul and the areas which we call the Inner Planes. You are exploring with a portion of your mind an area where you will journey later on at the end of your life, and your soul will retain that knowledge.

Within your exploration, you will gradually become aware at some level or another that there are Angels, helpers, guides, nurses, doctors, call them what you will, for whatever help you require, and you can also exchange conversations with them. Knowing all this you will find it less strange when you make that journey into the Inner Planes for the final time. You will know that they are there with you. You will see and feel them, and there will also be friends and relatives who have gone on before you waiting to welcome you. Your soul will ease gently from your physical body remaining approximately three earth days in the vicinity (while the silver cord detaches itself). Then it moves away into the Inner Planes to continue its journey through existence, through eternity, and eventually finding the metaphysical mountain.

If you find this a little difficult to understand, let us draw you a mundane parallel. Now, the first time you visit a new city or move to a new place, places are unfamiliar or seem to be far apart. They are difficult to find and it's easy to lose yourself as you turn from one block to another. When you've been a few times through the city, the distances seem to be closer and it doesn't take so long to get from A to B. The reason is you are now familiar with the city, you no longer have to look for signposts or to identify street numbers - you've stored away that information. Now your awareness is able to roam to other fields, thinking what you did yesterday or what you will do tomorrow - you've allowed your mind to detach - your journey is now automatic.

So it is in a similar way in the Inner Planes. Once you are familiar with the landmarks through your meditations, you can proceed further with your inner mind, soul, whatever you like to call it, much more quickly. There is no fear of the unknown because the situation is now known and recognized. A place where you have been before holds no fear.

The familiar is nothing to be afraid of. So make yourself familiar with the Inner Planes journey so that when that time change finally comes, as it will for all of us, you will travel happily, peacefully and knowledgeably. Knowing also that when Angel Azrael holds open the door and smiles at you and welcomes you in he is no longer the Angel of death, but the Angel of life.

So now we can continue to apply a similar sort of knowledge to our every day existence; recognizing our fears and whatever else we wish to dispense with by applying mind over matter.

Our minds are very, very powerful creatures. If it can create feelings of failure, then it can also create feelings of success which will be realized. Do you lack confidence in yourself? Many of us do, but having named these hang-ups which have been controlling you, you can now change the name to something much more positive, i.e. lack of confidence becomes self esteem which then becomes personal power and the start of your inner resources. Your success can be realized by producing a strong positive idea in your mind. Your mind will believe what you tell it. Negative tales will bring illness and pain, so don't deviate from your positive idea or doubt it in any way, and this visualization will crystallize and materialize this success. Just keep in mind "that which builds can also destroy", and you need to destroy all that unwanted baggage. And with all the powers that we have been given, without exception, the greatest is the power of thought.

Creating your own personal journal (for your eyes only) has given you a freedom of expression for your dreams and ideas. Study it well and understand that whatever you *believe* is the deciding factor in what happens to you. Your personal journal will take you far into your own mind and as you seek, so you build up a mental picture of how you see yourself and the Universe knitting together as one. Your goal at this present time is freedom from all mental, emotional and psychic tension. Change is the name of the game and as change is invariably hated (it disturbs the status quo), expect resistance from your mind at first as you clean your inner temple. Part of yourself will resent the fact that you have now exposed feelings you would prefer not to recognize, but another part of yourself will sigh with relief because you have found release in not having to hide them any longer. Just recall, we deceive ourselves because we're terrified to face up to what we fear inside ourselves. But it is when we countenance the turmoils, (become David to our own Goliath) accept the challenges and overcome them that we can then proceed.

So regroup. First thing each morning think "here is another day when I can create life anew". Leave yourself open to see and accept only things that have personal positive meaning for you. Having placed that new framework firmly in your mind, you can put out a call for your Angels. As your guardians, they will offer advice when you discuss your problems with them. Helping you to overcome negativities and doubts, and replacing them with the credits you have assigned to yourself is part of your Angels' duties. They are always available to give you ease of mind and will help to smooth the jagged edges of despair; for there is no doubt about it, life on this physical plane is a fight. It is a battle between the tendency of the mind to maintain a condition with which it is most comfortable, and the soul which needs experiences. But the Universe demands change. Trying to remain what you were yesterday is in conflict with the movement of this whole Universe. If you discuss this concept with your Angels, they will tell you that it makes strains in the fabric of Being. Therefore, we must flow with the Universe and pay minimal attention to that which has apparently gone before. We say "apparently", for the past has gone. It cannot be recreated except in our minds and even then it is not true, for memory plays us false.

Start with the here and now, then school your thoughts to positive with the idea that all in the future looks rosy. Put behind you the past negativities and obsessions. They no longer exist. Replace them with self-esteem and pride, and you will find your mental and emotional blocks will heal and your health will improve. So live in the present and watch the process going on underneath, quietly restructuring your life. When something new is introduced into your life, something else – perhaps even a combination of things must be removed. Change is a system of addition and subtraction in whichever area of your life it touches, so remember to make a note of these changes in the "change" column in your journal. As change takes place, you will become so preoccupied with this new state, old situations and upsets will be forgotten and memories will fade. These changes in consciousness enable you to exercise control over life's conditions and circumstances. Here is a very simple Cosmic Law to remember: have faith in yourself and the Infinite Powers, for you and IT are One. The less faith in yourself and the Powers, then the less your personal achievements shall be. Faith is stronger than belief. Belief is strong but faith is infinitely stronger. Faith is the foreknowledge of that which does exist. Belief is merely the fore knowledge of that which we confidently expect to exist in the future. You must grow your faith – see your small successes (achievements and change) and allow them to be the fertilizer which feeds the small seed of faith within yourself.

Chapter 5
Pulling Down The Power

s your depth of conversation with your Angels improves, they will explain to you that there is a correspondence between the macrocosm and the microcosm. There is a rhythm to the Universe and we are part of it. We and the Cosmos are one, so let's get you started on uniting yourself with it and getting it to work for you.

We know you are anxious to start making major changes in your life, but first you must learn how to really relax and also how to breathe and visualize properly. Yes, you touched on the edge of relaxation and visualization in chapter 3, but now you're really going to learn the works which will lead you into true meditation, and then the world becomes your oyster.

If you have already learned relaxation and meditation techniques, stay with what you know, and if you are comfortable with them, you can skip the rest of this chapter and probably the beginning of the next. But if you have never done this training, we urge you to follow and practice, practice and more practice of the lessons below before attempting to enter the true inner plane of your mind. Without them, you will more than likely experience great disappointment, because nothing happens and you'll say to yourself, "it doesn't work"; setting up a failure syndrome for yourself. Secondly you can meet some nasty "shells" from the lower Astral which can scare you into abandoning the next level of yourself.

So let's get started into relaxation. Many people understand the word relaxation to mean taking it easy, to lie around, or lazing in front of the TV with a few beers, pizza or popcorn. As an aspiring change maker, none of this is for you, your relaxation is the start of dedicated hard work.

As mentioned in chapter 3, you will need a quiet place where you can be sure that interruptions will not happen. You need a straight back chair in which you can sit upright, spine erect as possible but not poker-backed because the spine has a slight natural curve of its own. Make sure it is fairly well padded or your bottom will go to sleep and you'll be uncomfortable. Put your feet firmly on the floor, or you may cross your ankles if this is more comfortable. Lay your hands on your knees or your thighs. Take a look at the god-form posture of the Egyptian statues of the Pharoahs and imitate their position as much as possible.

Repeat quietly in your mind, "let go, let go" and see if you can feel the tensions draining away. You may not even recognize that you have tension until you can find out which parts of your body are tense, so the first part of relaxation is a deliberate attempt to find the various points of tension in your body. Start with your feet, be aware of them, how do your toes feel? Relaxed you think? Curl them up tightly until they almost hurt. Can you feel the tension? Now let go and feel them really relax from the pressure you have put on them. You should be able to feel the difference between tension and relaxation. Carry out this exercise on your feet until you can really understand the difference.

On next to the ankles, calves and knees, relax them, then tense them noticing where the tenseness is, then relax them again. On up to the thighs, the abdomen, the chest, the shoulders, the neck (you'll really start to notice the tension here), the throat, face and forehead. Pay particular attention to this upper part of your body, the scalp and hair above your brain. You'll find several areas up there that are tense, as we don't often use the scalp muscles and we tend to build up a habit of involuntary tension. Try frowning then letting go. Feel the tension which is constantly there? Try the back of your neck and across your shoulders. This is where a lot of tension is most of the day. You'll be surprised how much you can really let go when you concentrate on these areas, and note how good you feel when all those muscles relax and the tensions drain away.

These relaxation exercises are not going to be accomplished all in one session. You'll have to work on them until they become quite automatic, and some parts of your body will need more attention than others. Sometimes you will find that you've finally relaxed one part of your body and when you've worked on the next bit the previous bit has tensed up again, and you'll have to work on it once more!

This is the time to really pay attention to your body and ask yourself why you are tensing up. Go over your day bit by bit and you'll probably find the answer, then let the whole thing go. Remember once something has happened it's over and done with, so drop it over the side as if it never existed. Old Chinese proverb says your happiness depends on your reactions to your daily environment.

You must be wondering if all this relaxation stuff is really necessary. Yes, it is. You are teaching yourself self awareness (as opposed to inner awareness which comes later) and also making inroads to controlling your mind and body. Remember we mentioned previously that your mind was controlling you? This is the start of you taking control over your own little universe. You may think it is boring right now, but persevere, it will become an automatic process later on and you won't have to think about tensing and relaxing your muscles. They will do it themselves as soon as you sit down at your selected time, because your mind has already been trained to obey and to recognize your meditation time. We'll tackle meditation time shortly, after you have learned to breathe and visualize and direct the white light. Yes, we hear you say you know how to breathe or you wouldn't be alive, but like most people, you breathe in a shallow fashion. The only time you really fill your lungs during the day is when you take a deep breath and sigh, or you take a big breath to calm yourself before you face the boss. Now, taking that big breath fills the lungs, calms the nerves and helps the muscles to relax. That's in your physical world where you are facing a situation which you would subconsciously like to control. Now you are going to learn to deliberately control your breathing to lead you eventually into a meditational state. This type of breathing must only be put into operation when you are moving into your meditational state. Otherwise, you'll end up with an oxygen overdose which will leave you very dizzy and uncomfortable.

The idea with the breathing is to increase the supply of oxygen (without overdoing it), to feed the physical body, completely filling and emptying the lungs. At the same time, we breathe in the prana (the manna from heaven) to feed our spirit. The deeper you drop into meditation, the slower and more rhythmical your breathing will become and it will take care of itself.

We are not normally aware of breathing as it is so automatic, but we want you to be aware of what you are doing and what is happening. When you inhale, let your stomach come out, blowing it up like a frog. Expand the lower part of your chest, then raise the middle part of the chest slightly contracting your stomach, and finally lift and expand your upper ribs. You should now be full of air – but don't strain. That's important. Pull in as much air as you can, without strain. When you breathe out, just reverse the process. Let your ribs deflate, relax them and pull your stomach in.

This should be all one continuous movement and you can watch your breathing in action by touching your fingertips together just by your navel. As you breathe in, your fingertips should move apart and come together again as you breathe out. Breathe in through your nose and out through your mouth and note your breathing will be slower than normal.

Now, having made yourself aware of what happens when you breathe, take a full charge of air counting up to 8 as you do it, hold it in your lungs for a count of 4, then let it out through your mouth for a count of 8. Make sure you keep your throat relaxed. If you find the count of 8 is too much for you, adjust to suit yourself, try with 6 counts in, hold for 3 and then out for 6. If it is still too much for you drop it down to 4, hold for 2 then out for 4. The timing is not important, the breathing exercise must be comfortable for you, and once you've found your comfort level, do the exercise 6 times.

At this point, you might like to go back to your journal. Take a fresh page and make a note of difficult tension points which need further attention, and also record your reaction and awareness of your breathing exercises. Awareness at this stage is most important as you will need it when you start on your meditations. Listen also in your mind for whispers from your Angels. As your breathing improves the blood flow throughout your body, so your inner self responds to the cleaning and your contact will start to become much clearer. Listen for messages, suggestions or just a feeling of plain joy and upliftment.

Now we will start in on visualization of the White Light, directing it through and around your body. You will need your journal to record your bodily experiences and the awareness of your five senses throughout this exercise.

You did some very nice visualizing in chapter 3, painting a portrait of your Angels. Now you are going to extend your power of visualization to draw down the White Light and circulate it around your body. Have you spoken to your Angels lately? If you have (and we're sure you have carried out your daily communication), they must be very proud of your progress and delighted at the closeness developing within your contact.

Now, if you have religiously carried out the previous exercises of relaxation and breathing, when you activate this power and direct the Light, some of you may actually catch a glimpse of your Angels. We're not making any promises here, but as you have been reactivating the clairaudient power you were born with while you have been talking in your mind to your Angels, some of you will have awakened your clairvoyant powers as well. This means you will be able to see your Angels. One of the perks in training your mind and body is that these powers (the Eastern teachings call them Siddhis) which came with you when you were born are opened up again. And you can use them if you are interested in them, or you can just ignore them and they will lie dormant again. These byways can be very interesting as some of our students found. Some developed psychometry, telepathy, crystal ball gazing, even past life readings and healing powers. If you want them, they are yours for the developing.

In the meantime, let's move in on the White Light. You know the steps by now. First the relaxing, then the breathing. Now, when you've got the rhythm going satisfactorily and you are nicely relaxed all over, take your attention to the top of your head and visualize a big ball of White Light sitting over the top of you. In your mind, see the rest of your body sitting comfortably in your chair. Now bring that White Light down all around you as if you were standing underneath a shower. Keep thinking and seeing it, pretend you are having a shower. Lift your face up to it, feel it, let it ping gently on your skin, feel its velvet touch, its gentle

54

warmth. Gradually, in your mind, firmly direct this gorgeous light across your throat, then across your shoulders and down into your arms and into your finger tips. What do you feel? Remember it.

Now pay attention to your chest, see the light there and gradually move it right down throughout your body; down, down and into each leg, through your thighs, knees, ankles and into your feet. By now, if you have taken your time in controlling the light, you should be experiencing a warmth and a tingling feeling stealing over your body.

Now sit there quietly for a short while and let this light completely envelop your body, pulsing through you and feel the warmth getting stronger. Are you at the stage where you can let your mind roam a little yet keep the light moving? Good. Then on to the next stage. If not, keep practicing, it will happen.

Keeping your shower energy moving, direct your attention to the top of your head once more and make contact with that ball of light. Imagine a wide shaft of light studded with seven diamonds placed at intervals down the front of your body and see it vibrate from the top of your head down your body in a straight line to the soles of your feet. Direct this light shaft up the back of your body, up your spine until it joins once again with the ball of light at the top of your head. Now you'll have to juggle this, keeping the whole thing moving, both the shower and the shaft. Annoying isn't it, how one or the other gets away and you have to chase after it and put it back in position? Persevere, one day you will look at it in amazement and see that these two are working in tandem, and by golly, you'll feel the power. While you are handling this, gradually train your mind to observe the constantly changing nature of your bodily sensations and your thoughts. You see, once you get the hang of moving this energy around, you will feel different movements within your body. Your mental and emotional faculties have been stimulated. Your thought power will feel different. Another interesting little exercise while this is going on is to try to catch the thought bubble when you find you have a thought coming to the surface. Stop the thought process immediately, but hang on to what you have in your mind. Then trace the thought back bit by bit, until you can find where the thought first came from. What triggered it? It's a fascinating and most illuminating mental training exercise, and the results of this and what sensations and/or communications you have received during your White Light exercise should be duly written up in your journal. In future times, when you look back at your journal jottings you will recognize just how far you have progressed and how much you have achieved physically, mentally and spiritually.

While you have been practicing the previous exercises and improving your mental and physical state, you have, of course, been putting aside time to confer with your Angels. By now, there should be a much closer connection, and you should be able to detect their energy patterns when they are close by. The next exercise will bring you into much closer contact with them.

Not again, you say, not another exercise. All I wanted was to talk to the Angels! Why more exercises? Because these are things you do every day without even being aware of them – and remember, the name of the game of walking the spiritual path is total outer and inner awareness. So now you are going to learn how to be aware of your five senses which you will need to put into operation on every mind level as you climb the ladder of Light. Learn this lesson well and truly, because you are going to use your five senses in the next chapter when you visit the next level of your mind as you move into the Astral Light.

Before we start in on this lesson, take a few minutes to really look at yourself and see how you feel and act now compared to what you were before you decided to make your changes. Have you noticed that your life force has become magnified? Your friends and co-workers probably have and some of them may have commented on the change in you. Notice that your thoughts are quickened, your senses are heightened and the powers of your mind have expanded so that the physical, mental and emotional bodies within you begin to work together in harmony. You should be feeling new heights of ability, happiness and spiritual well being. And if you are really making progress, it's quite likely that you will feel a prickling sensation in your skin as if it is peeling and dropping off. It's called the sloughing of the skin, it doesn't hurt and it's nothing to worry about. Some of you will also feel an itching in the middle of your forehead. The itching of the third eye which is situated in your forehead (the pineal gland) – sometimes it's called "the tickling of the ant"– it's the opening up of your sense awareness. These physical sensations are signposts along the way indicating your progress and you will experience others as you progress upwards.

Let's move along now to examine the images of the five senses. Seeing, feeling, smelling, hearing, tasting, how much of them are you really aware in your day to day existence? We'll run through a material example, think about it as you read.

You are off to work in the morning, you look at the clock (seeing) and vaguely register it is time to leave to catch the bus. You slip into your coat and gloves, (did you feel the material?) and kiss your partner goodbye (did you smell his aftershave or her fresh soap smell?). Did the slam of the front door register with you? Can you still taste what you had for breakfast, or did you clean your teeth leaving your mouth with a fresh minty taste? Were you aware of the sound of your footsteps as you moved along the sidewalk to the bus stop? Did you notice your breathing, especially if you were in a hurry? Waiting at the bus stop, were you aware of the other people? What did they smell like? What did the air smell like? A pleasant or unpleasant smell? When you saw the bus coming, were you really aware that it was the bus you were waiting for, or did you take it for granted because that was the time it always came? Did you hear the tires on the tarmac? What sound did it make as it drew up to the sidewalk and opened its door? What did your legs feel like as you climbed the steps? What did your nose register as you moved towards a seat? Did the driver thank you for your token as you dropped it in the box, did you smile at each other and feel any sensation when you said "good morning", or did you not bother with a greeting? Lots of things to think about in the matter of awareness, eh? See how things pass us by because we do not use awareness. It's just total routine without being really alive.

Let's do another one. This time we'll take a mental journey into awareness activating all five senses. When we teach these awareness sessions, we like to make them interesting and fun rather than the old routine of repetitive taped music and waiting for something to happen. Using known situations intrigues the inner mind. It likes to be involved and it co-operates much more eagerly. So off we go. We'll go to a garage sale, they are always fun.

First, you must do your breathing and relaxation exercise and get yourself into your visualization mode. Ready?

Now, imagine you have just arrived at the place of the sale. See yourself parking your car, feel your foot on the brake pedal, feel your hand as you set the brake and turn the key to shut off the engine. Remove the keys, open the door, climb out and shut the door behind you and lock it. Feel within yourself everything you have just done, put your tactile sense to work and really experience it. In your mind, stand still for a moment and look at the people around you, really see them. What are they wearing? What are they carrying? Do they have expectant looks on their faces? What are they handling and how? Do you hear what they are saying? What else do you see about them? Register it in your mind and remember it so you can make a note of it in your journal when you have finished your exercise.

Now, move forward towards the tables. Examine the goods carefully. Pick up a few bits and pieces here and there; feel them. Ask a few questions of the person running the table. Listen to the sound of the voice. Ask yourself if you are interested in the item. You are? Then pay the money feeling the sensation of the coins in your hand. Wander along to other tables listening to the conversations of the other people around, the sound of the children, the yapping of a dog. Did a cat just brush by your leg? Did you bend down to stroke it, and were you aware of it purring to you in answer to your gesture? Can you smell the car fumes of the other people who have just driven up or driven away? Be aware within your mind, make your mental pictures come alive.

Look at all the things you've bought. How are you going to get them all home? Think. First of all you'll have to make room in the trunk of your car. In your mind, go through the motions of getting out your keys, unlocking the trunk, pushing some junk to one side to make room for the rest you've just bought. Now comes the test, is it going to fit? That chest will probably go at the back, the coffee tables to one side, the bookcase might just squeeze into the front, and that box of books? Well, they'll just about go in but the trunk won't close. Now, where did you put that yellow twine? Think about it, it's got to be there somewhere. Are you feeling and experiencing this as we go along? If not, go over it again and again, or make up your own scenario for this is an important part of your learning process; not only for spiritual development, but for your very necessary material needs. Ah, there's the twine. Oh nice, here comes the owner of the garage sale to help you with your goods. What does he look like, what is he wearing, how does he walk, what does he have to say? Remember, they are always cheerful when they are getting rid of their junk and you've just paid for it! The pair of you load the stuff inside, you handle the yellow twine, feel its coarseness, the oiliness of it. Be aware of the smell of it. Then the man takes it from you, ties down the trunk for you, gives you a wrapped fruit drop to suck on the way home, shakes your hand, and says goodbye. Now, smell your hand. He's handled so much stuff today your hand doesn't smell too good now. Never mind, unwrap your candy, hear the sound of the paper as you unwrap it, feel its texture, see its color, pop it in your mouth, and experience the taste as you drive home to get washed up.

Gently bring yourself back now into your own reality, back into your room, and if you've made a good job of your visualization you'll really think you were there at that garage sale. Take a few minutes now to write up in your journal the whole experience of this mind trip expressing everything that went on within your five senses. This is the difference between your outer awareness (the bus trip) and your inner awareness (the garage sale) which you have just experienced through visualization.

Would you like to take another mind trip? This one is slightly different, but do it on another day, you've done your work out for this day.

Before you sit down in your favorite quiet place, get a piece of paper and a fat pen. Not one of those thin things, but one you can really feel, something like a marker but with a writing point. A "Sharpie" is an excellent choice as it fulfills all five senses. Before you start work, examine the pen closely and remember what you see.

All set? Get comfortable, breathe and relax yourself, and as soon as you are ready, pick up the pen and close your eyes. Feel the weight of it in the palm of your hand. Is it heavier at one end than the other? Is it smooth all over or ridged towards the writing end? Examine it carefully with your fingers and remember what it feels like all over, then see yourself in your mind handling the pen.

What color is it? Does it have more than one color? How are you holding it, like a cigarette between your fingers or is it lying in the palm of your hand? Are your fingers curled around it? Which hand are you holding it with? Make a detailed exploration of the pen within your mind and hold on to every sensation which you will record in your journal when you've finished this session.

Still holding your totally relaxed state, open your eyes, and pick up your piece of paper. Examine it, feel it, is it rough or smooth? Does it make a noise when you rub it with your fingers. Now, write a sentence or two on the paper with your pen. Note the sound of the pen on the paper. Does it remind you of anything?

Quickly now, what thought came to mind when you wrote your sentences? Cast your mind back step by step till you can catch the bubble of thought that made you write those words. Examine the bubble - follow the connection upwards as the thought begins to form into an idea (notice the thought form you have created?), and the consequence of that thought is the words you have on paper - here you see cause and effect in action. Do those words relate to anything in your life right now – perhaps something past or future? Analyze it, see if the words have a connection anywhere within your self profile. What force inside you urged you to write those particular words? Again, examine carefully and if you see a connection, make a note of it in your journal.

Did the sound of the pen remind you of anything? Did you notice the smell of the ink as you wrote your words? If not, smell the paper, you should still be able to catch a whiff of it. Did you have a thought, even a fleeting one, as the sound or smell took place? Do the thought bubble exercise again, see what you come up with and note if it ties in anywhere with mind and/or emotions. Quite a mind opening exercise, isn't it?

Have you noticed that whenever a cop stops you for speeding or whatever, he gets out his pen and licks the point? So go ahead, do the same thing (did you have a reaction at this suggestion?) and note the taste (yuk) and the sensations the action evokes. Then write it up in your faithful journal.

And what, you say, shall I do with all these exercises and information you've handed me? First of all, set yourself a purpose, a goal and a destination for that goal. Next, recognize you've been handed the simplicity of drawing to yourself everything that you've always wanted or needed. In fact, everything, no matter what, is always there within the Universe for you to reach out for. It's an exchange of energies - yours for ITS. The reason it doesn't happen all that much for a lot of people is that there is very little force put behind their thought forms.(Remember we mentioned force and form in chapter 2). What they have imagined just disperses like the clouds leaving nothing behind. And secondly, people do not believe the actual simplicity of aligning themselves with spiritual energy to receive the bounties waiting there for the taking. They are under the impression that because they have a physical body, they are required to work hard and accept all the ills and frustrations that they consider fate is handing them. Not so. The old magicians and metaphysicians used to say "inflame thyself with power"(or prayer, which is the same thing) and that's exactly what you are doing when you are in your altered mind state of relaxation; pulling down the power and using your five senses. So, quite simply, if you want it, whatever it is, feel it, see it, taste it, hear it, smell it, have faith in it and you'll get it. Just accept the fact that everything there is, has been and will be, is there in the Universe and always will be and so is your share. Be as a little child. Have faith and walk hand in hand with the Universal energies. That's really all there is to it to start the changes in your life. Simple? Yes, but very effective.

As we come to the end of this chapter, we reach a parting of the ways for those readers who do not wish to go any further up the Path of Enlightenment. You have learned a great deal, made many changes in your life for the better and now it is your choice, or rather the choice of your soul, for IT is the one who knows whether you are ready for the next step. Nevertheless, by getting in touch with yourself, altering your life style, and activating your inner self, you have just experienced your first spiritual initiation. Your Angels also know what your next step will be and it matters not to them or your soul if you feel you are not quite ready. They are your friends and will always be with you whatever your decision, so stay firmly in touch with them for the rest of your life. When you are ready to take the next step up, your Angels will hold the Ladder of Light for you.

BOOK 2

STARTING THE MIND WALK

To All Those Who Seek the Divine Union

Search for the light of reason
Seek in the light of spirit
Dig in the turmoiled stirrings
Of those teachings far beyond
Sleep for the sound of trumpets
Hark to the heav'nly throng
Hold to the evening glory
Feel for the angel's song
Hold to the touch of knowledge
Fly to the clouds above
Float in the arms of spirit
Bask in the warmth of love
Then when the trumpets clamour
Loud in the end of time
Brave are the divine soldiers
As the last long clarions chime.

By
Lt. Louis F. Hellerman W. W. One Fighter Pilot

Born December 24, 1898. Shot down in flames August 15, 1917.
Given to us by automatic writing May, 1970.

Chapter 6
Entering the Astral Light

aving made your decision to step on to the Path of Enlightenment, we say to you "Welcome Aboard". From here on, through to the end of your life you will experience some of the most remarkable happenings that you would never ever have dreamed of. Your life will change so radically, and within your new blissful existence you will wonder how you ever lived the life you're about to leave behind. As you move step by step along the Path, you will understand how limited is the average view of the physical world and why so much pain and unhappiness exists in so many people. You will be able to stand back and see this from a different view point. And the love and understanding you will now absorb from the Planes, you will be able to share with others at a later date. So let us move along the next few steps of the Path.

You've learned a great deal about mind control in the previous five chapters and throughout the rest of the book, you'll put it to work (with marvelous results) as you step your way through each of the altered states of consciousness.

Now, you are not doing anything weird, wonderful, strange, or dangerous, because you have done this type of thing before when you have been in a daydream state. Think about it, perhaps on a hot, lazy, hazy summer day when you let everything drift away and you entered that relaxed state. Your mind was at ease, and you were thinking about other things. You were picturing things or events you would like to have happen. You altered the state of your outer conscious awareness. It often happens when you get into this dreamy state, but you tend to dismiss it instead of remembering what went on in your mind. It's really amazing where our awareness can take us when the mind is even slightly moved to one side.

Geof had a most fascinating experience one day as he was traveling home on the bus. He said it was hot on the bus and he was a little tired so he relaxed back in his seat. The next thing he knew, he was a twelve year old boy traveling in a coach on his way back to boarding school and feeling miserable about the whole thing. He was aware that this was taking place in England, his name was Phillip Townsend, that he was traveling from his home in Nottingham to his school in Birmingham. The coach and four horses was stopped at an Inn for a change-over of the horses. He said he could feel the uncomfortable horse hair seat beneath him, hear the horses snorting which were beside his coach. The thing he recalled most was the startling sight of the hessian on the horses' backs which were steaming. "I'd never even thought of that," he said. He could also hear the hostlers talking and joking, and see the clothes they were wearing. As he realized the time framework was in the seventeen hundreds, he found himself back on his own bus, and the whole episode had taken only a few minutes. To this day he says when he thinks about it he can still get a sense of the reality of that episode of a past life.

Another interesting example was when we were holding a Past Life Seminar one weekend and one of the girls described her experience of being a soldier on a battlefield. She described the dead and the injured, the flies hovering over them, the dreadful stench of blood, and the fact that her armor was too tight and biting into her flesh which inhibited her sword arm. She also recalled that the armorer had deliberately made her armor too small as they disliked each other. It all seemed so real at the time of this happening and she said, "I'd never given a thought about the idea of blood having a smell. It was quite revolting."

The difference between these two events is that one (Geof's) was uncontrolled (he just let his mind drift and entered a state of changed awareness), and the objective of the seminar was a controlled state of awareness which also took our student back into what seemed to be a past life. In both cases, the five senses were activated, a set of conscious processes took place, passive in Geof's case and active (set in motion and controlled) in our student's case. Now you can see that the five senses are the gateways to the mind, and how important those exercises were in chapter five.

Throughout the previous chapters you've worked your way through self-observation (introspection) and solved various problems through silent speech (communication with your Angels or one of your other selves) or through mental pictures. You are probably aware now that your analysis of your outer consciousness was an important task where you have cleared out a lot of unnecessary debris. Hopefully, those distorting experiences of the past have been dropped over the side and you've learned to program your mind to select the choices which benefit yourself, and accept the consequences of your actions knowing that you are totally responsible for them – no one else.

Having understood all this, you are now ready to take the next step up, your first true Mind Walk, and enter the Astral Light; the mental plane, controlling and directing your awareness as you have been previously taught. Taking your own Angels with you, you will be introduced to the Angels of the Astral Light who will help you across the Mind Walk as you encounter another part of yourself as we mentioned in chapter 3.

You know the routine by now in getting yourself into another mind space, but before you do that we suggest you find a notebook or another part of your journal which you can open up to become a dream book. After experiencing this fascinating adventure, you are likely to have many dreams. Be aware that your mind (ego) will try to take control again at first, and you will have to subdue its egotistical tendencies to be the boss. (A suggestion here is that you listen well to the words of ego before you dismiss it. It preaches a false doctrine and by reviewing its ideas and expressions, you may find what the true self knows to be true and keeps quiet about.)

Another suggestion which you may find very helpful is to prepare some incense or light a sweet-smelling candle, and have some soothing music playing very quietly in the background. The incense or candle will activate both the sense of smell and taste as its odor will get down the back of your throat, and the music will stimulate your sense of hearing. If you are using a candle, the flickering of the wick will turn on your sense of seeing even when you have your eyes closed.

All set? Then off you go. You are in your quiet place comfortably seated, relax, relax, do your breathing exercises until everything feels right, then start pulling down the power of the White Light. As you let that power swirl around and through you, feel your five senses awakening and totally let yourself go. Let go, let go.

In your mind, feel yourself gradually moving outwards, then see yourself walking down a pathway towards a gate at the end. (Some of you will actually see another part of yourself move out of your body – "bi-location" – and you will be able to experience this exercise as if you were watching a movie. Others will find all five senses are involved). As you reach the gate, you will see your Angels waiting for you. The gate swings open and you step forward into a beautiful garden of trees and flowers, hedges and bowers. See the asters and Michaelmas daisies in a blaze of different shades of purples, blues and magentas. The marigolds with their orange coats and the roses glowing amber and pink. The smell of the flowers is intoxicating and they gently perfume

70

the air. You marvel at the array of different colors as you gaze at the jasmine, the daffodils, the sweet smelling stock, the honeysuckle and other flowers you have never seen before. You watch the honey bees going from flower to flower and the utter peace of the whole garden is a totally new experience for you.

Your Angels smile as you look around in wonder as you suddenly realize that the flowers, trees, bushes, all fauna and flora are all living, speaking, communicating consciousnesses. And you are somewhat taken aback when they greet you, especially the exotic butterflies who sit on your hand and rest in your hair. Look carefully at the gardens and you will see the garden Devas at work tending the plants, talking to them as they continue along with their tasks row by row. They too will greet you and show you some of the plants – the volunteers they call them – which have come from another Universe or a parallel time to be with their relatives.

Your Angels take you by the hand (hopefully you can feel the contact) and walk you slowly towards the courtyard of a mansion you can just see in the distance. As you arrive, you see a great marble fountain. There is a wide shallow pool and the fountain stands in the center. Note the cool shadows and the fat white doves strutting and preening on the flagstones. Squirrels come to greet you, standing up, hoping you have something nice for them and you form the thought that you would like to feed them. Instantly, you find a bag of nuts in your hand and the squirrels hop onto your arms and shoulders while you dole out their feast.

Remember what we said earlier about thought forms? When there is force behind the thought, whether positive or negative, something will happen. Your thought form here was created with love straight from your heart with a desire to feed the squirrels, and the nuts appeared. All the Inner Planes are created by thought. Much was mentally created eons ago by other budding initiates and this has now become actual reality in all Planes. Whichever mind slant you take yourself into, you will encounter many fixtures, but some of this reality has changed as the thinking patterns and understandings of the human race altered as time progressed. In chapter 10, you can experience the museum and see how and why these changes have taken place. What you have seen and experienced so far, and what you are about to experience are fixtures. For instance, you saw the fountain, you saw the doves and the squirrels, the flowers, the trees, the grass. The river which you are walking beside is also a fixture. See the punts on the water, hear the fish say, "Mind me, mind me," but the people in the punts who reside in this Plane will eventually change as their awareness and understandings change. Their energy pattern will alter and they will move into the next Plane of awareness as they shuck off another layer of "physical" body. And once again, we'll explain more in chapter 9. Right now, it's time to move on further and if you look just beyond the courtyard to the door leading into the mansion you will see a round vibrating ball of light.

As you move closer towards this light, it develops into three distinct personages. You are about to meet the Angels of the Astral Light. Manuel, Giel and Casujoiah stand before you and greet you with love. An all encompassing love, the like of which you have never experienced in the earth plane. In which way you "see" these Angels will depend entirely on your own mind set. Remember how you created the portraits of your own Guardian Angels, how you chose your own style of personage? Your mind will automatically do the same with these Angels and it really matters not what you think they look like, because they are really intelligences, energy patterns, as we have described before, and you are merely clothing them with your own ideas so you will recognize them again and again, each time you visit.

Having been introduced to them, your own Angels wander off to rest or play and the trio of Angels now take over. You are invited inside the mansion where you are shown many lecture rooms where classes are taking place on a variety of subjects, taught, not by Angels, but by humans who have passed on, who enjoy teaching, have something to impart, and wish to continue in their previous profession. The people who are absorbing the lectures are earth people like yourself. Some in a physical earth meditational state, some in their sleep state, and some have already passed over having experienced the death state. But all have chosen their subjects and they are thoroughly enjoying them. You too, may do this if you wish once you have been shown around this Plane.

Off again, out into the Astral Light, the light which is so soft and bright, but you do not need sun glasses to shield your eyes as the Eternal Spiritual Sun will not burn, but just gently warm you. A peaceful walk by the river now, where the willow trees bow down to the water and share their energy with the lovers who sit beneath, and the sunlight shines through the evergreens bouncing its light off the ripples of the river. If you stop and gaze into the water, innumerable fish will rise to the surface to greet you and communicate. Do be polite and answer, they will understand you just as you have understood them. Strolling onwards, peeping in the arbors as you go past, you will see groups of people deep in discussion, other groups enjoying a picnic. Out in the open, you will encounter athletic games being played, children enjoying themselves; some looked after by their nursemaids, others in a group for story telling time. Further on in the distance you see a bandstand, hear music and see people enjoying the concert. Your trio of Angels inform you that concerts are always taking place, ranging from opera through country and western to jazz, depending on what the awarenesses are expecting and desiring. In fact, the Angels are rather amused as they detect your disbelief which you are trying your best to hide, but they understand and

73

accept because they experience this with all new visitors.

Perhaps, they say, you would like a visit to the market place? Stunned by everything you have seen so far, you merely nod your head and continue on. And what a sight you see. The market place is actually a meeting ground for minds. Here you will experience all sorts of philosophies from beings who are standing on platforms all spouting their own "truths". This is somewhat like Hyde Park Corner in London, England on a Sunday morning where you find people on their "soap boxes" as they are called, expressing their own opinions about everything under the sun, and crowds of people gather round listening to them. Here is a similar gathering with a diversity of beliefs. The Christians talk about their God for they know they have the truth, and the metaphysical ones tell about the energy of the Universe without a man made God. The astrologers give their opinion and the non-believers heckle and shout. Others are complaining about the Astral Police and the Guards (they really do exist) who occasionally move them on because they are making a little bit of trouble. They say the Angels of the Astral Light should be on their side and chastise the police and guards, but the Angels are having no part in that.

You sit on a bench with the Angels and watch, in total disbelief, at the world around you. But you say, this is so similar to my own earth world. And indeed it is to a certain extent, but remember this is what thoughts have built in this particular Plane, just as you have created your own thought forms and built your own reality in your earth world. Later, as you progress along other Mind Walks, you will have such esoteric experiences that they will often be too difficult to bring back into your waking state. Each awareness level is different, your Angels inform you. In fact, they say, there is another level "beneath" this one where people who have passed over reluctantly have brought their possessions with them. Of course, it's all in their minds, but thoughts are things and it's an interesting place to visit. And we have the time to do so, for time does not exist.

Without knowing how they did it, your Angels have whisked you into this other Mind Walk where you see houses, shops, streets, people sitting on their balconies enjoying their beers. Others watching television, listening to their radios, conversing over the fences, attending to their gardens where they grow their fruits and vegetables. Cars stand on the street, people walk down the street carrying their shopping, taxis wait on corners for a fare, buses wait for passengers. You don't believe it? Neither did we at one time.

Many, many years ago when we first got into metaphysics, we went to a lecture where the speaker was talking about people who built their houses when they passed over, created shops, sidewalks, anything that was a replica of the place they had just left. If they couldn't take it with them, they weren't going to go, was their philosophy. And as they couldn't stop the going, they recreated it on the "other side". We thought it was the funniest thing we'd heard in a long time, and spent quite a while giggling over it every time we thought about it. We were searching, suffering from Divine Discontent. We took this course and that course, weekends here and there and nothing appealed to us until we met up with an interesting group. Then things took off for us and we found our own Paths. It was at this time that Geof developed into a trance medium (now called channeling), bringing through some very interesting entities. Not Angels, but people, seven of them, who had originally had earth lives and now had passed over. They gave us much information of the life on the "other side". Geof also learned to do automatic writing and some of this written information has been used in this book, along with the metaphysical lectures given us from the other six speakers.

Our spiritual entities helped us develop our own meditations, and once we got the hang of moving into different Mind Walks indeed we found people did create the earth plane they had just left behind, because they were still so attached to it they couldn't let it go. We watched, we talked to them, we listened, and over the years (and we're talking nearly fifty), we met some of them again in other levels as they progressed from their mental creation of the earth plane into a finer "body" of awareness. So, introduce yourself. They won't know if you have passed over or are just visiting. They won't see the Angels who accompany you because they (the Angels) vibrate at a faster rate and cannot be seen by them as yet. So feel free to walk and talk and ask questions.

Eventually, your trio nudges you gently reminding you it is time to move upwards again, as there is one more visit they wish you to make before you leave. Before you can ask the next question, you find yourself, and the Angels of course, standing in front of a building which claims to be the Library. A library yet! But how did we get here, you ask the Angels. Thought, my little earth being, they reply. Remember, everything is thought once you leave your clay body behind. Think where you want to be and there you are with no trouble at all. And laughingly they say, "How do you think we got stuck with the notion of wings on our backs? Mortals couldn't understand the power of thought taking us anywhere, so therefore we had to have wings and fly like the birds."

By now, you are probably tiring a little, which the Angels will detect, so your visit to the library will be somewhat brief, but what a sight it is. The room is flooded with light and warmth, but not a warmth that overheats you, just a welcoming warmth where you feel you could stay forever. A monk comes to greet you and bows to the Angels of the Astral Light. He is introduced to you as Friar Dominik. He has been here for 4,000 years, you are told. He is still searching for his man-made god with whom he spent his earthly life. So far he has not found what he thinks his heart desires. He does not yet understand that everything he thinks and writes about comes from Universal Mind, which is the undifferentiated Source of All, and being part of this himself he is his own god. There is no other. He cannot come to terms with this yet and until he does, he will remain where he is, looking after the books he loves.

There are books galore around the walls. And where the walls are free they are embedded with jewels of different colors which gently pulsate stimulating mental energy patterns and giving off healing rays. Little nooks and crannies are filled with people who are studying or reading. Tucked away in a corner in a large armchair, there is a young girl with a black cat sitting beside her. On her lap is a large story book from which she is reading out loud to her cat. The cat is totally animated with the pictures, pawing each page before it is turned, sometimes it nods its head in understanding. This is Sheltie, you are told. She is twelve years old and here is her cat Tinker Bell. They were both killed in an air raid during the second world war when a bomb fell on their house. Sheltie had Tinker Bell when she was a tiny kitten and has always read her stories and shown her pictures from her books. Tinker Bell, like other animals here, can now communicate and the two of them have wonderful conversations during their reading, walking and exercise time. Later, they will be stacking returned books to the shelves, as part of their work. Tinker Bell, of course riding on the trolley directing Sheltie to the correct aisle.

Looking across the room, you see two young men working at computers – computers yet! – and you shake your head in wonder. The Angels laugh at your confusion and introduce you to these identical twins, Lionel and Elliot. They were at university in 1919 when the influenza epidemic, which circled the world, finished their earthly existence. You think you saw one of them at the Market Place earlier, and now you want to know what they are doing at the computers. If you people can communicate by thought processes, you ask, why do you need computers? Yes, you did indeed see one twin earlier at the market place, the Angels say. He was there making notes of the ideas which are thrown out to the crowd by the "soap box people", which could be very useful to the Archetypal people. He brings them back to the library where they are discussed, and suggestions are made to make them useful then they are sent Angel mail (A.Mail!) to the upper levels where they are gratefully received. "Nice for them up above" the twins say,"they have new computers which they keep designing. We have to make do with their old ones because they are too mean to give us ones they have just designed. Ah well, we can wait, we have the rest of eternity."

The Angels tell you that the twins will soon be leaving the library. They are brilliant fellows and on the next level, the Creative plane, a group is waiting for them to join them. The twins are just about to slough off their "old mental skin" and move to new pastures. As you wonder why it has taken them so long to move up, you realize you are no longer talking out loud but communicating with the Angels through telepathy. In your mind, you hear that there is much to learn, and the understanding of concepts invisible to mortal minds takes some while to be absorbed. Spirituality, healing and therapy walk hand in hand down the avenues of all levels of the Astral Light, and the twins have been taking classes in many subjects, for time is not a factor. Their level of understanding of the spiritual world, Universal Mind, now enables them to slough off their layer of a grosser frame and they will move into a more refined one where further teachings and understandings will take place. Having reached the top of their "ladder" in this Plane, they will be at the bottom of the next level and start their climb all over again.

With all you have seen and heard on this journey, you feel yourself fading in and out, and your Angels tell you it is time for you to go back to your normal physical state. As you thank them for their time, love and energy, you find yourself back at the gate with your own Guardian Angels, who are gently guiding you through and onto the path you came in on.

Gently, gently now, start to feel yourself awakening, feel the chair beneath you, become aware of the room just as you left it. Now recognize that you are back in your own time with a wonderful experience inside you. How long have you been away? It feels like days, but in your reality you've only been away for forty-five minutes. Sit relaxed for a while before joining the hustle and bustle of your home life. Jot your experiences down in your journal and keep them to yourself. In your mind, you hear your Angels tell you the maxim of the occult world: **KNOW**: yourself with all your strengths and weaknesses. **WILL**: Have the will to take control over your mind and body. **DARE**: to put your new found knowledge into action. And **KEEP SILENT**: Don't boast of your success or try to change others. Example does the change. If you try to share your experience with others who are not walking the Path, they will criticize or make fun of you, and you may become convinced it never happened. Remember how we told you about belief? This is your own special time, experience it over and over again whenever you wish. It's real, it's true, and the more you do it, the more adventures you will have.

Chapter 7
Chakras And Symbols

When you took that Mind Walk in the previous chapter, it's quite possible that you had different experiences to the ones you've just read about and expected to happen. What we have described is a combination of our own experiences and what we experience is due to our own mind sets. You have your own set of beliefs, values, truths, understandings, attitudes, ideas – the complexes of the whole outer shell of your personality; that which shaped you in your earlier years. If you've done the earlier workouts suggested in "Making a Profile of Yourself", you'll notice that your ideas, understandings and acceptances have changed from those previous years. If you take a look at yourself now, you'll see that they have changed again as you've worked further into the book. So your present mind set, which stimulates your mental and emotional faculties, will bring different encounters and this inner reality is yours alone. As we mentioned before, we have many different selves and each time you turn a mental corner, you can walk into another state of mind. The more you carry out these exercises, the more states you will discover and your mind set will constantly change. What you believed yesterday is no longer valid today. Your inner and outer awareness has had a realization (an "aha") and replaced your belief with something more acceptable (for this present time) until something else comes along and changes your understanding; belief and truth. These changes are most fascinating as you walk the Path, gradually shucking off the grosser frame of each level as you come in contact with it.

The previous chapters and exercises covered visualization, concentration and actualization. These are the framework on which rests all your future work and your climb up the Path. They are now embedded within yourself. They are an automatic happening each time you sit down to meditate, and they will lead you quickly into your chosen mental state. Which means, of course, hooray, no more lessons, just practice, practice, practice. So, let's move onto the next level; meeting more Angelic Beings. Here you can learn to work with more energy patterns which will take you further into other realms.

Do you recall that wide shaft of light studded with seven diamonds that we mentioned in chapter 5, when you were directing the White Light throughout your body? These seven diamonds are known as Chakras, the spiritual focal points, and we receive energy into our bodies through them. They are psychic dynamos, centers of super-physical energy, and your use of them can bring about almost magical experiences.

Chakras can only really be known through meditative experience, the basis of which you have learned in previous chapters. It is the vehicle for reaching a particular state of mind. In this path of self-awareness, it's not a case of what "turns you on" as before when you examined your feelings, emotions and reactions, but more of what "turns you off". You'll know if you have reached this state and you are making progress, because distractions will show up, always in your meditation time. Other people feel the need to put their garbage down the hatch or drag their garbage pail to the curb, put their empty bottles on their balcony. Trucks will stop outside your house and leave their engines rumbling. A neighbor, who rarely comes will choose this time to visit – they'll find a million ways to disturb you. This is your testing time to learn to block out all sounds and totally concentrate on what you are attempting to achieve. Try not to react or let anger and frustration affect you, you'll only draw unbalanced force towards you. Let the sounds wash over you and they will drift away and so will your mind.

Each chakra has its own energy pattern and its own color scheme, used for different purposes, both spiritual and material. Each chakra looks like an inverted flower bud pointing downwards. When it is pierced by the directed energy which flows through it, it folds in on itself, closes into a tight ball, then blossoms out. Its petals then unfurl and face upwards, and here you have new power, new experience and new vision. You can solve your own immediate problems by application, detachment and focused meditation, setting these psychic-dynamos in action. Choose whatever you would like to work on from your previous lists or something which has recently come to mind that needs attention. Follow the leadings of your inner self. Let the wisdom flow freely and you'll make progress. In fact, if you build well in this Plane, your physical body will reflect the well building. As you work with and come to understand the power of the chakras, you will discover the hidden portion of your spiritual self, with further awakening of your higher consciousness.

These seven chakras are known as follows:

1: **Base or root chakra** – located at the base of the spine, pointing down towards the feet and legs. Its associated color is olive green, its energy relates to the physical body. The understanding of sexual energy arises here as well as your need and love for the opposite sex. Your contact is the Angel Aiel.

2: **Navel or Sacral chakra** – located just below your navel. Its associated color is red and its energy relates to relationships, friendships, and emotions which can delve deep into the subconscious increasing your awareness further. Your contact is the Angel Tual.

3: **Solar Plexus (sun) chakra** – located at the solar plexus or above the navel. Its associated color is yellow and covers the nervous system, your willpower, determination and your sense of destiny. Your contact is the Angel Sagras.

4: **Heart center chakra** – located at the center of the chest region. Its associated color is blue. This energy center deals with unconditional love (one of the hardest things to develop), expansion of the inner self which gives and expects nothing in return. Compassion develops here. Your contact is the Angel Ol.

5: **Throat chakra** – located on the throat. Its associated color is orange dealing with communication. How do you express yourself, your needs and your understanding of the needs of others? Your contact is the Angel Voel.

6: **Third Eye chakra** – located in the middle of the forehead. Its associated color is lavender. Here you develop a knowingness, a greater depth in your visualization. Concepts and ideas occur to you which you put into practical application for the benefit of yourself and others. Your spiritual self takes a great leap. Your contact is the Angel Pasiel.

7: **Crown chakra** – located above your head from which emanates the White Light you've used previously. If you ever touch these energies, even for a very brief moment, you will experience an area of total bliss which cannot be described in words. To reach this wonderful stage takes courage and determination and a lifetime of dedicated daily meditation.

It truly is the Path to Enlightenment, but we have other ways and means to tread the spiritual path which eventually joins up with this energy pattern. Your Angel contact has no name, it is just the Angel of the White Light.

Success with the use of the chakras depends entirely on the detail of your visualization. The techniques which you learned in the previous chapters are brought fully into play now and you'll use them more and more with each further chapter. Developing the energy of the chakras is useful for your everyday physical/material life. Putting this in order is necessary on each level of your existence (i.e.: relationships, mental stamina, health, happiness, prosperity) – anything that you need as mentioned above in the chakras. Bear in mind that your physical body is the temple for your spiritual body, and your spirituality grows along with the development and understanding of yourself. The more you meditate and the more Mind Walks you take, the further your development and understanding will be. When you get to know each chakra energy and what it can do for you, anytime you have an upset (as will always happen no matter how spiritual you think you are!), you can activate this energy to guide you. Don't concern yourself with spiritual things, "as above" will take care of itself as you take care of the "so below". The balance of both spiritual and material is important to your well being.

In Part One of this book, you were guided to examine yourself, your past existence and to understand or just accept your experiences. Now, with opening up your energy centers, you will delve more deeply into yourself. Perhaps facing other parts that you were not ready to face previously. These are the deeper demons of self – which we all have. When you walk the spiritual path, you will come face to face with them as you experience what is known as "Daath" – the little death. Death of the unwanted, unnecessary elements and unbalanced force of the darker side of yourself. Later, when you have accomplished this, you will be rewarded by being guided between the Pillars of Boaz and Joachim (the gateway) towards the Temple Veil.

Chakras are fascinating things to work with. When you are using them, don't do the Mind Walk – that's to take you into other realms of existence. This chakra work is purely for other cleansing rituals which you'll carry out time and time again whenever you need to. Just do your relaxing, breathing, then the White Light. Having decided which chakra you wish to work with, concentrate on that area and visualize a small spinning wheel. As you gradually make it gain speed, apply its color, then think very clearly in your mind what you wish to achieve or

85

change within yourself. You will find this energy therapy eventually removes energy blocks. Say, for instance, you are still blocked by feelings of anger, shame, confusion or depression. For a start, concentrate on chakra number 2 and bring the red color to your spinning wheel. Are you still dealing with feelings of anger? Ask yourself why you erupt, fly off the handle and see "red". You'll get your answer along with the beginnings of transformation. Your beliefs, thoughts, emotions can and will be altered, being replaced by confidence, self-esteem, mental and physical energy, and feelings of joy and usefulness. As we mentioned in the earlier part of our book, and we're repeating again here and probably will further on, it's your own response to people and your environment which causes problems. Eventually, you learn not to react, but to ignore whatever is going on and to mold your own universe to your liking.

As you continue to explore your inner self, you'll discover and start to recognize patterns, and realize that you're repeating those same patterns over and over again: habit patterns, behavior patterns. Examine carefully the pattern you're in right now and how you got there. A trip to past lives will show you how you established a certain pattern in the past – eons ago (see chapter 12) – and that pattern will be a recurring theme throughout your lives. Also, recall that patterns associated with recall and memory are engraved on the molecules of your physical (mental molecules). Exploring yourself makes it easier for you to change the structure of undesirable mental molecules by setting up a regular pattern to learn to control your mind. Also, to establish a habit pattern of positive thinking and speech helps you to create thought forms which influence your own material universe, as well as this very plastic spiritual universe.

Within your newly recognized and established patterns, you will find the Angel of the chakra you've chosen who will guide you towards the path which helps you to go forward, or (if you have made an error) to suggest you start again. Other solutions will come to you if you relax your mind and let them drift in – courtesy of your chakra Angel. If you do catch a fleeting glimpse of this Angel energy pattern, it will be clothed in the same color as the chakra you've chosen, and, once again, just as before, you'll know if you've made contact – things will feel different. And so will you each time you go through another cleansing ritual. No matter how many levels you climb, you'll always find some aspect of yourself that you've just recognized, don't care for and needs removing.

Once you start using this energy therapy, your dreams will take off. Did you start a dream journal earlier? If not, it's time to start one now. Having activated the chakras, the next step is adding symbols to your work and then your dreams will really be impressive, because your mind is a creature of symbols.

Some people actually do dream "true" (our son does), which means they dream actual occurrences which are to take place, or even of a past event which seemed to have little meaning at the time. But the dream shows the dreamer how the past and the "now" have (or is about to) come together. Lucky people.

Most of us dream in symbol form which we have to interpret. Some years ago I (Maiya) had an interesting dream which answered a question I had asked myself. Remember, I have been walking the Path for many years and I was just getting over one of those soul slumps (which you will also encounter) where the spiritual skies seemed to be made of brass, and my soul had been resting under a Bo tree for a long while. My meditation periods were dull and unproductive, and I'd asked myself if I'd inadvertently stepped off the Path. Was I really climbing my spiritual mountain, or was I just kidding myself? (Yes, I still doubt myself occasionally, and after all the wonderful experiences I've had, I should know better!)

Anyway, in my dream, there was a long street in front of me which suddenly went up vertically and I found myself driving a car right to the top. When I reached the summit, I turned in my seat and looked back at the sheer drop behind me and my dream mind said, "Look how far you've come". This answered my question, my soul stirred itself into action as the spiritual skies lightened and away we went (my soul and I) on up the mountain again. I found that most interesting, as the dream also touched on a fear I'd been trying to overcome. For years, I had refused to drive because I had failed my driving exam twice, but passed on the third go around. Deep down, I was somewhat ashamed of my failure and because of that, I used the excuse that I might cause an accident as I was an inexperienced driver. I really wanted the freedom of being able to drive, and I knew perfectly well that I was the only one who could build my confidence, but I still avoided it. My dream, on this second level, pointed out that I was in control of myself spiritually and experiencing the freedom the spiritual realms give. And if I could drive myself through the difficulties and challenges of climbing the spiritual mountain, I could transfer that confidence and freedom into my material world. I recognized all this but still backed away from it until destiny forced my hand and I had to face my own fear. Geof had become very ill and lost partial sight in his left eye, and he was unable to see properly to drive. With my heart in my mouth I took over the wheel again. I gradually built up my confidence and now I have my desired freedom in both worlds. Destiny works in unique ways and in this case it forced my hand.

This brings us to a point where we can say that we, too, still battle with some of our inner demons of self. Gradually overcoming them. Some taking years and some being forced to face (like Maiya's), so don't expect to get rid of your hang-ups all at once. No doubt, like us, as you get rid of some, you'll find some more. Just keep plodding. Transformation continues to take place bit by bit, and you too will be able to look back and see how far you've come.

Having digressed a little, let's get back to symbols of the mind and the dream state. Dreams are a clearing place for the information we have taken in and stored away during our waking hours. Sometimes we use it immediately, our dream symbols come up that night or within a few days. Otherwise, the information is stored away until it can be fitted into some form of pattern acceptable to the set of our minds.

Our minds are like computers and we continually feed information into it at random, without thought and without categorizing. During the sleep state, sorting and filing takes place and we are presented with dreams – information in symbolic form – which helps us to deal with our every day conscious world.

The more you have trained your mind and become its master (as you've already learned), the more powerful your internal computer becomes and the more effectively you will function on a daily basis. Dreams offer us ways of solving problems which seem to be unresolvable on a conscious level. When the limitations and inhibitions are removed in the sleep state, the mind investigates its own storehouse of images and also delves into what Carl Jung called the "Collective Unconscious" where all information appears to be stored and is available to all of us. The other term which is used for this is Universal Mind. And as you enter the different levels of this power house (you have already visited some), you will recognize the basic patterns of this energy which you adjust in your dream state to fit your own experience. Within these different levels, are many dimensions and aspects of self, and the interpretation of your dreams also depends on the understanding of yourself. Hence, all the previous exercises and the cleaning of the inner self.

As we have suggested previously, the more control you have over yourself on the conscious level, the more you have over your external world. Then you are in control of your own destiny. Your dreams will indicate your strengths and purposes as you further climb your spiritual mountain. A dream journal is now an important adjunct so you can monitor your own progress. Within this journal, you will learn even more about yourself as your dreams expose the hidden parts of yourself.

Find yourself a notebook and leave a big space in which to recount your dream with as much detail as you remember. Put the date at the top. Now leave another big space on the other side of your notebook to write the results or the happenings of your dream when it comes to fruition. Again date the results. Sometimes you will have the same or very similar dream at another time. If you have the information in your journal of what that previous dream brought forth you will know what to expect. Then consult the dates – when the dream occurred and when the happening took place (what the time element was between them). Then you will know when and what to expect with a recurring dream. Here you can learn more of yourself by remembering your reactions and emotions regarding the fruition of your dreams. It's worthwhile making a column in your journal noting your response so you can counteract any unbalanced force (i.e. anger, spite, jealousy etc) next time the dream appears. On the other hand, if your response is a positive one, you can use it and double your benefits.

We can't tell you what your dreams will be about – these depend on your circumstances, environment, emotional and psychological conditions. From this, your mind will set the scene for what needs to be brought to your conscious attention and from that you must decipher the symbolism. Look for the theme of the dream. Then other aspects can be defined and further interpretation of the images can take place.

A good dream book can also be a help – a starting point from which you may be able to develop the insights of your dream. Many years ago, I (Maiya) had a dream in which I was looking at a wallpapered wall depicting cornflowers. A very pretty wall, but I could make nothing of it. The dream went no further but I noted it in my journal and looked up the basic interpretation in my dream book. The wallpaper interpretation suggested I may be wanting to make changes in my life, but to search diligently first. The flowers suggested that something new and fresh was about to come into my life. I still couldn't make sense of it but jotted down the information. At that time, we were very busy people. We were editing an astrology magazine, writing articles for other magazines, seeing astrology clients on a daily basis. Geof was writing another book and he was doing many radio and T.V. shows. I was also preparing a number of paintings for an exhibition. How was something new going to come into my life and where was I going to put it? I didn't have enough hours in the day as it was, and I was trying to interpret this dream on a purely personal basis. It hadn't occurred to me that Geof might be involved.

CBC had recently given him a new show, an early morning show. And I mean *early* as it was then connected to one of the Atlantic provinces who were hours ahead of us time wise. This meant he had to be in Vancouver (B.C.) at the T.V. station around 5am, and we lived on acreage about an hour and a half away from the city. After some months of this early rising, Geof suggested we sell the house and move closer in to the city. So off we went on a house hunting expedition. Here was the start of the predicted changes (and to search diligently). After a few weeks, we found exactly what we were looking for and moved in. A few months later, I was in the little bathroom brushing my teeth, gazing at the wall while contemplating the article I was writing when it dawned on me I was looking at that same wall of wallpaper with the cornflowers on it that I'd had in my dream so long ago. My dream world had dug it out from somewhere in the future and given me the information, but I had to wait for it to come to fruition. So here was the new and fresh (an environment)for us, sadly without a quiet private acreage.

Another dream that used to occur fairly frequently was when we were teaching a variety of metaphysical concepts. One fellow was constantly taking lessons, and he always had a big bag of complaints. It got to the point where my dreams picked up on this, and the symbol of the cross kept popping up. I noted each time the cross appeared in my dream, "whatshisname" singled me out for a good moan. I was now prepared in advance for this and could finally take it in my stride without feeling annoyed and irritated, which was how I had reacted before. This usually spoilt the evening teaching session as other sensitive students picked up on my feelings. So you see how dreams can work out when you take notice of their symbolism.

So what is symbolism and how can symbols improve both our spiritual and material lives?

Chelas – students of the metaphysical disciplines have been using symbolism in the shapes of triangles, circles and squares for centuries in the practice and development of visualization. The use of symbols links the physical and the metaphysical worlds. And the understanding of them conveys the realities of the inner worlds to your consciousness.

We use symbols in our daily lives, which we take for granted and rarely think of them as symbols. If we give them any thought at all they stand out as directions. We recognize driving symbols: the yield sign, the railway crossing, the winding downhill or uphill curves. Then the bigger signs at the side of the road showing the gas station, a place to sleep for the night(the picture of the bed), the police station, the farmers market(the farmer with his fork), the grocery store (the basket on wheels). We see them and they all enter our minds automatically, without conscious thought. We are all aware of mathematical symbols that we learned at school and still use in every day life: the plus, the minus, division, equals, square root, parallelogram and the triangle, circle and square. These last three symbols (when used in meditation) will take you on a journey into the deep mysteries of the mind – which is where we've been heading all along. Recall, this book is about developing your own spiritual journey.

These mandalas (symbols) represent the cosmic forces, and some of these lesser divinities you have already experienced in your previous exercises. The use of the mandalas is two fold. You can meditate on the force itself to bring you transcendent spiritual experiences, because these images will speak directly to your unconscious mind. Here you will find a truly mystical sense of oneness with the force it represents. Or you can discover different aspects of your own inner potential of which you are not yet aware. With this realization, deep inner transformation will gradually take place bringing changes in your outer world.

There are many symbols that can be used for both material and spiritual purposes (particularly the Tarot cards), but for now we'll use these three: the square, the triangle and the circle.

To your inner mind, the square represents a firmness and a stability. Recall how we talk about four square? Here you can use this symbol very effectively in the organization and restructuring of your life. As you gradually clean out the useless and obstructive portions of yourself, you will see how the square (when meditated on) can put solidity and a sense of structure into that space you have opened up. When you charge and energize that square with the force that you have previously learned (strong visualization), you will set up an electro-magnetic strain in the Astral Light, and whatever you request or need to fill that gap, will happen.

At the end of chapter 6, we mentioned the four axioms of the occult world – Know, Will, Dare and Keep Silent. Two of them come into play here. When you have decided what you need to fill that gap (Know), you now put your magical Will into action. This is the force (the visualization), which brings the form into your life. Always remember in your work that Will is the most important of the four axioms. In our material world, it is referred to as will-power which requires a lot of hard work. But you know now how to put your mind to work for you, removing the word "hard" from your vocabulary.

There are three colors used for these mandalas: red, yellow and blue. Meditate on a yellow square for all your practical affairs including business and money (although your financial affairs should be improving rapidly as your spirituality develops). As you bring the White Light into yourself, change your energy field to yellow and visualize strongly the yellow square. Results, both spiritual and material will follow.

The triangle in its highest sense represents the Trinity when its point is uppermost; bringing a sense of Divine power when meditated on. When pointing downwards its red color will bring power and authority into your life along with prestige if you are ready to handle it. For instance, having been in your job for a number of years, you feel it is time for a promotion to come your way. You desire a position of authority, yet a step up seems to keep passing you by. This is the time to put the triangle to use.

To help you concentrate on your desire, draw yourself a red triangle, point down which will bring the power into your material world, then settle yourself in your quiet room. Do your breathing and other exercises to relax yourself totally. Then gaze at the triangle without blinking for as long as you can. Gradually close your eyes and visualize the triangle with as much imagination as you can muster. Within the triangle set a scene of yourself in the position you want. Add lots of detail just as you did when you created a portrait of your Angels in the earlier chapters. You see, when you develop your magical Will, creative imagination is its counterpart. And these two working together will bring you whatever you need in both a material and spiritual sense, for these also work in tandem. You can also mix any of these symbols, they don't necessarily have to be used singly. If, with this previous example, you feel a little apprehensive in thrusting yourself into a position of authority (wondering if you can really handle it), make yourself a yellow square and place your red triangle in the center and get on with your creative visualization. You'll develop a confidence and stability within yourself and when your new position comes to fruition, you'll be able to handle it successfully.

And now for the circle, blue in color, which will bring you back to health if you're feeling under the weather. Are you having a little bit of trouble, arguments or upsets? Use the blue circle and create a picture of happiness and pleasure. Feel the vibrations of joy stimulating your senses, and a change of atmosphere will take place. The secret to making all these changes happen is a very simple one. Within your creative imagination MAKE THESE SCENES LIVE.

Having experienced the value of these energy patterns to alter your life, you will find the following chapter offers more guidance and adventures into the spiritual realms and more understanding of other levels of existence.

Chapter 8
Meeting the Angels of the Solstices and Equinoxes

s you go deeper into yourself, you will come into contact more and more with the natural forces within the Universe. But first, you will find that you are becoming more introspective, looking back (sometimes with amusement, sometimes with a twinge of guilt) at how you handled people and situations. You'll remember the people around you when you were very young, and you'll have a flashback to your companions and associates. Then you'll fully understand that these were the people who influenced not only yourself, but how you thought about the rest of the world.

Some of these people you learned to trust. They helped you develop a sense of your own worth and taught you a sense of cooperation and sharing. From others (who perhaps had a greater influence over you), you learned not to trust, even yourself. To doubt your self-worth and value leads to feelings of insecurity. Cultural trends in your growing up years shaped the way you thought and felt and even now, in your older years, hostile thoughts from your own ego will continue to surface and they will have to be slapped down.

As a true Chela of the Mysteries (if you weren't, you would not have gotten this far into the book), you have understood that you have to breakdown and destroy unworthy characteristics and attitudes to be able to expose the beauty of your inner self. The weeds, debris, small stones and dust – psychiatrists call these "neuroses" – which previously clogged your inner mind, have gradually been dissolved through your exercises and meditations. Your awareness and your subconscious have started to work together.

You have self-initiated changes in your life, but also accepted others which have been imposed on you through external circumstances. Have you reacted to them in a totally different, yet resilient and courageous way from earlier years? Whatever your response, it has changed both yourself and your future path. And so it shall be as you continue to tread the Path, whether in a physical, material body or after death in your spiritual/soul bodies. You will always be your own alchemist searching for your personal nugget of gold; always discovering more of your inner being as you reach out for that Divine Communion.

We're proud of your accomplishments. Your reward for your years of practice and hard work is your second initiation. This one takes you into the Temple of Wisdom where you are introduced to the Angels of the Equinoxes and Solstices. These Beings are of a higher vibration than the ones you've previously met. Their duties are concerned with the tides of the Universe and the four elements: Fire, Earth, Air and Water. They are also connected to the four cardinal points: North, South, East and West.

Astronomers often refer to these points as the "four cardinal moments" in the year. The summer solstice in June is when the earth's North pole points most directly at the sun which gives us the longest day. The winter solstice in December is the shortest day when the pole points most directly away from the sun. The spring and autumn equinoxes occur when the sun crosses the celestial equator, then night and day are of equal lengths.

These cardinal points are linked to four very powerful Universal Tides which metaphysical seekers know as the Tattvic Tides.

These four great tides are of much practical value. They are most interesting to work with and help us tune in to the ebb and flow of Universal energy. Of course, these tides are continuous within the Universe itself – not just four times a year as we know them. If you could see them (and one day you may just catch a glimpse), they look like great rolling waves of energy. They flow over and under each other, bunching into particles which seem to have a slight sound like musical notes, then break into bits of light, and join together again. If you can catch it, you can flow through this consciousness and briefly become a part of it. It's a fascinating experience which words cannot express, and each of you will have a different experience. When Geof had a couple of experiences, he felt as if he was riding on a surf board on the waves and he remained exhilarated for most of the day. Mine is somewhat different. I know when I've been there even if I do not recall anything in particular except the tranquility of my soul. But physically, I wake up feeling a little dizzy and slightly nauseated due to the rolling energy. But then, being a sensitive water sign, I get seasick on a water bed! Nevertheless, I look forward to my visits because I return with a tremendous amount of creative energy and I can write for days without running into a stumbling block. For you? Who knows. As we said before, we all have different responses and you have that excitement to come.

At this juncture, we would like to mention that there is a lot of confusion and contradiction regarding the meanings and workings of the Tides, Equinoxes, Solstices and their symbols. At the turn of the century when metaphysical teachings were in their vogue in book form from leaders of Occult groups and Lodges, some of the so-called "secret" teachings were deliberately altered, which misled aspiring students who wished to learn on their own rather than being under the thumb of a group. Errors – deliberate or not – have been compounded when they have been copied incorrectly, until they have been accepted as gospel. They still continue in mixed up form today. Particularly on the internet where the contradictions are very obvious.

What we are offering you is what has worked for us and our students over the years. If it, or some of it, does not suit your mind set or you are used to a different method, don't use it. Go your own way and use what feels right for you. Use what you want or need and dump the rest – that way you will develop your own philosophy.

Nature has its own patterns and its invisible side speaks deeply to our souls. The sky at night, when the bowl is full of stars, a sunrise, sunset or brilliant full Moon can make us catch our breath at its beauty making us more aware of our inner being – our higher self – oversoul or whatever you would like to call it. And we feel closer to the Divinity. At the turning of the seasons, not only do we set a pattern for our lives, but animals also recognize the Tides – bears hibernate, birds fly South for the winter.

We, as human beings are usually only aware of the outer cyclical changes called the Equinoxes and Solstices, but the Tattvic changes go deeper inside ourselves bringing us the recognition of our constant building and destroying – the continual transmutation of our lives. We can harness this powerful energy of each of the Tides by knowing what we can use them for, rather than working against them.

Tide number 1 which starts with the winter solstice in December is called the Tide of Destruction. It seems a funny place to start, doesn't it? But it is the clearing out of all unwanted stuff, like hopes and dreams which never came to fruition(thanks for the memory!). Plans which you made in the previous few months which never materialized. Anything or anybody which brings imbalance into your life. So expect your future plans to be well tested during this three month period which more or less ends at the start of the Vernal Equinox in March.

We recently went through our Tide of Destruction in a number of different ways, so here's an example for you. In the late August, towards the end of Tide number 3, we bought a house which needed some finishing – we enjoy this type of thing – and we were just about to move in when a tornado went through the area tearing off the roof, breaking windows, damaging the balconies and screen doors, but the sellers insurance company was taking care of the damage. This was to our advantage as we would have had to do these repairs anyway, but we had to live with the inconvenience until the damage was repaired, which took many months. When the fall Equinox and Tide number 4 took place in September, we laid out our plans for the alteration of the house and started in on some much needed finishing before winter set in. In December, at the start of Tide number 1, Geof had a bad attack of stomach flu and was sick for a number of weeks. In February, he was outside snow blowing with the machine when he had a heart attack. He had another attack the following day. The flu bug had strained his heart. We were sent from one hospital to another for this test and that test and he seemed to be recovering nicely, but he had to take things easy. That put on hold our indoor winter plans for painting and decorating. The following month, just before the end of the Tide of Destruction, he had a stroke which hit his brain damaging his speech pattern and causing him to partially lose the sight in his left eye. More hospitals, more tests and this was the time when the driving was given to me as I mentioned in an earlier chapter (and yes, I'm still doing it and strangely enough actually enjoying it).

The outcome of this Tide of Destruction was literally a destruction of all our plans for that house. We were forced to put it on the market as Geof could no longer deal with the acreage or the snow blowing. All our machinery was sold along with what we no longer needed. The rest went into storage and we ended up in an apartment (yuk!) until we found a suitable house. At least he didn't have to snow blow!

After Tide number 1, this Tide of Destruction, comes the Vernal Equinox in March, Tide number 2. This is called the Tide of Planting and Sowing. The ideas, ideals and plans that have survived after the onslaught of that testing ground will be good and solid. Plant these mental seeds with love, visualize their outcome, adore them and tend them often, just as you would in your spring garden and see them blossom into something fruitful.

The third tide which comes at the summer solstice in June is called the Tide of Reaping. You should now be able to reap what you sowed in the previous tide. Gather in your harvest, the fruits of your hard work both on the material plane and the spiritual plane. These two planes must balance each other. Body and soul must work together and this is most important. We reaped our harvest (cash wise) when we sold our house. And our spiritual benefit is healing time for Geof which is slowly taking place. More time for relaxation and meditation and more time for writing, being together and caring for each other instead of seminars, lecturing and teaching.

The fourth tide, the one we are in at the time of this writing, takes place in September, the fall Equinox. This is the Tide of Formulation, of making plans for the future. Examining your past and deciding which were your successes and which became failures and moving on from there. Evaluate what went on before and note that, within what look to be failures, you will actually find success.

We swam against our Tide of Destruction and used its energy (cash) to our benefit. We are making further plans right now. We fancy moving to another province, but we are hampered by continual medical appointments for Geof. Especially now that he has just had laser surgery to his eye, and he needs the follow up appointments in three months time in case it needs redoing. A number of different plans we have laid out, and we shall see how they work out when the Tide of Destruction comes about in two months time. We'll probably be able to share them with you later as it will take somewhat longer to finish writing this book. A most interesting time awaits us as we also know we are about to reach a destiny point in our lives; often called a Fork in the Road which will result in total and complete change for us.

This description and our experience of the Tides should help you in working with each one as they come about. If you look back to the previous year at the times of the Equinoxes and Solstices and remember what went on in your life, you can tie your experiences to the Tides themselves and you will be more aware of their influence. Using the Tattvic Tides to set your future goals (providing they are realistic), will put them in motion and bring them to fruition much more firmly.

Having discovered what these Tides can bring, there are also symbols which go along with them, aligning themselves with the four seasons. Three of these symbols you've been introduced to in the previous chapter, so you know how to work with them. These symbols stimulate the powers of the imagination which you will need to use more and more as you climb further up the Path, so note them carefully. You will need them to contact your Angel energies because these Beings respond only to the symbol and color with which you have clothed them.

Use of these symbols will help you deal with the circumstances of both your inner life and your everyday outer life. What is happening here is that your subconscious mind is sorting and classifying the happenings of life into a pattern. Recall, we mentioned habit patterns? Subconscious is a great pattern former. Left on its own, it is undisciplined and waddles about willy-nilly without much of a pattern to guide it. With the aid of these symbols, you will devise your own mental pattern where you can call on the powers and forces of the Universe. This of course, is where your previous training has been directing you.

The Equinox in March which heralds the spring season relates to the astrological sign Aries. Its element is Fire. Its cardinal point is East. Its color and symbol is the red triangle. Angel Nathaniel looks after the Fire element and Telvi directs the Equinox.

The summer Solstice around mid-June when we have the longest day, we think of as the beginning of summer. This Soltice relates to the astrological sign Cancer. Its element is Water. Its cardinal point is South and its color and symbol is a silver crescent. Angel Hamal tends to the Water and Abrid brings in the Solstice.

The autumn Equinox bringing beautiful fall colors in mid September belongs to the sign Libra the element of Air. Its cardinal point is West. Its color and symbol is a blue circle. Angel Baciel circulates the Air while Meleyal balances the Equinox.

Finally, the winter Solstice in December, the shortest day, is the sign of Capricorn the element of Earth. Its cardinal point is North. Its color and symbol is the yellow square. Angel Sochiel tends the Earth and Cetarari guides in the Solstice.

The symbols you've used previously, hopefully understood and from which you have received benefits, are being reinforced here to open up further paths into the Inner Planes. And you will be introduced to the silver crescent and the indigo (or black) oval.

At one time when we reached this stage with a class, one student said that all we seemed to be doing was working with material, earthy things and sorting through emotions and reactions. "Where's the spirituality in this?" she wanted to know. The answer to this question is, the spirituality is inside yourself. You are constantly purifying and cleansing your inner self and cleaning the Path ahead for your soul to reach the Oneness. You are a material being surrounded by an emotional and somewhat vicious world to which you would normally react in a negative way, as we've talked about in previous chapters.

Now we have a question for you. How would you cope with your everyday life if you had your head in a spiritual cloud all day long? You couldn't deal with it. You would make no progress and have no awareness of what's going on around you. You'd be so stupefied, you'd probably walk under a bus without even seeing it. And, being so unbalanced, you would have given nothing back to the Universe, so you would have to reincarnate and do that stretch all over again with extra penalty, because you'd built more Karma for yourself.

So yes, it seems like you're dealing with earthly things. And the testing ground of your spirituality is the increase in peace, harmony, friendships, love and your relationship to the outside world. Your finances, stability and worldly goods have also increased, removing your fear of the future. As has your recognition of your world and maybe your world has recognized you. How else do you know you are becoming a spiritual being? In your meditation and quiet times, occasionally you will be filled with such an indescribable feeling of pulsing light(s), maybe of different colors or the room will glow and bounce with light balls or stars. You will be so suffused briefly, and you will know with such a certainty that you have been touched by the Ineffable. You will never forget. And each time you think of that marvelous happening, you will glow inside.

The only way to touch and stay in touch with that Wonder is to keep sloughing off the earthly layers bit by bit through your Inner Self exercises, and staying in touch with your Angel energies.

Your thought forms and strong visualization builds a lighted pathway – a channel – through which the Angel energies enter your own personal sphere and you'll feel that power. You are also likely to be drawn by invisible streams of spiritual energy into the deeper aspects of the Planes when you will be inducted into a Group Mind of the Inner Planes. We'll talk more on that in a later chapter.

Now we will put together the Tides, the symbols and the seasons and you will note that some of your previous exercises in the use of senses and visualization will be put into action.

With the Vernal Equinox opening up in the Spring, everything starts to come alive. Animals awaken, plants begin to show their heads above the soil and your own knowledge of the Divine, which you have gained through previous study, starts its surging emotions in search of further spiritual illumination. In your meditation time, make your visualization extremely strong. See Angels Nathaniel and Telvi clothed in a rich red which warms you as you gaze at them. (Note you are using the senses of seeing and feeling.) How you see them, how you clothe them, what kind of portrait you mentally draw is up to you. You learned how to do this in chapter 3, but this time make it really strong and powerful. What these Angels respond to is the shape and color of the symbol – the red triangle. Communications and contacts in the higher planes are done through symbols and sounds; nevertheless, you will understand in your mind what you are given. Visualize an open fireplace inside your triangle. See the flames, smell the odor of the burning wood, hear it crackle and pop as it settles further into the grate. Do you see pictures within the colors of the flames? We did when we were children. Bask in the warmth and glow of your triangle and subconsciously listen for extra sounds or sights.

These Angels are concerned with the regeneration of Universal life(hence the Vernal Equinox). Their element – fire – purifies, transforms and re-creates(remember the story of the Phoenix?). We all have a phoenix inside ourselves which helps us to overcome change and to handle with ease the periodic destruction of the previous Tattvic Tide (no.1). Whatever you have left from that Tide of Destruction, offer it to the Angels who will tell you how to use it. They will give you a great deal of help if you are aspiring towards a higher unity. They will also offer solutions to any conflicts you may have in your daily life, and motivate you towards your next step.

If you put two triangles on top of one another, one uppermost and one inverted, you have a representation of fire and water. Water is also a symbol of regeneration helping to sublimate anger or over activity within this fire element. If you count the points, these two triangles become a six pointed star (Solomon's Seal or the Star of David); a symbol of the human soul, of the physical and spiritual joined together in harmony to create wisdom, but also of ambivalence and equilibrium. Meditate on them and see what you get. The triangle is recognized as an occult symbol representing a bringing together, or an upward surge toward the ultimate source of enlightenment. It's also the Greek letter delta, the mathematical symbol for change or transition. If this is your desire, work on the triangle and whatever you want will come to fruition.

With the Summer Solstice comes duality, the heat of the Sun and the welcome drops of rain to feed the soil. Here is a symbol which you have not used before, the beautiful silver crescent. Symbolic of the Moon, it represents liberation and freedom from the Karmic wheel and the occult side of nature. Water is the element and Angels Hamal and Abrid consider this to be their paradise as they watch things come and go.

This crescent shape of water stands for transformation and regeneration, but in the shape of wearing down and rebuilding, rather than the burning up of the previous element. Somewhat like the Moon in its stages of building up, becoming full then waning and disappearing, so do the stages of the human body follow suit; the appearance and disappearance of the earthly form.

Each Tattvic symbol can be used as a doorway into one of the different dimensions of yourself. Within this silver crescent lies the first step of the Great Work – namely dissolution (1st matter) – the destruction of attitudes, ideas and the complexes of the outer shell of the whole personality. This corresponds very neatly with your first chakra which has allegiance with the Moon and your sexual energy. Just because you are heading towards being a spiritual being, don't avoid or despise your sexual needs. Understand that the joining together of two human bodies and the enjoyment of each other is the earthly representation of the connection of spirit and material. At the base of your first chakra lies what is called the "sleeping serpent", the Kundalini energy. When this serpent is aroused through the understanding of the joining of spirit and material sexual energy, all chakras light up including the Crown chakra giving you a glimpse of the Indigo egg (sometimes called the black egg) whose symbol is the oval. This is force pure and simple. The wisdom of the deep and of the great mysteries, a magnetic force representing transformation and a sense of the eternal. If you put the two halves of this crescent, one on top of the other joined together they become the oval, the egg of the world. Silver on the bottom, indigo on top and here again you have the concept of "As above, So below"; the relationship of the two opposites. What will you get out of this on a spiritual level? Meditate on it. Each to his own.

Naturally, you will be reaping the material benefits of the seeds you sowed during the previous Tide, and in your meditations strongly visualize Angels Hamal and Abrid in their silver cloaks.

Feel the silkiness of the material and the softness of the lining. Catch the glitter as the sun bounces across their shoulders and shimmers on the waters beneath their feet. See the animals which surround them also enjoying the summer day. Hear the drone of the bees and the insects flying and singing. See the greenery of the summer months, feel the grass beneath your feet, visualize a gentle rainfall and feel its moisture on your face. Put out your tongue, catch the raindrops and feel refreshed, then turn around and admire the beautiful rainbow. Can you imagine the pot of gold at the end of the rainbow? It's there as a symbol of illumination and salvation. In olden days, the Alchemists were actually trying to change lead into real gold, not recognizing that the gold was within themselves. The changes and purification you are making within yourself is changing your physical lead into spiritual gold.

As you put your goals in place, see yourself moving through a day in your life, enjoying it, moving it towards sundown and sunset and then see yourself relaxing under a beautiful silvery crescent Moon. Listen for the tinkle of bells in the distance or faint musical notes as you dream the next stage of your life. Absorb the silver energy of the Angels into your whole being and let the hidden side of this symbol start its work.

The fall Equinox in September heralds the move towards a cooling temperature and its symbol is the blue circle which you've used before. Its spiritual meaning is the return to Unity from the multiplicity of the previous symbol.

Angel Baciel moves the air through the leaves of the trees while Meleyal decides which leaves will drop and which will remain a little longer until the old man with the scythe comes with his winter touch. See these Angels clothed in blue (the color of the sky). Note the autumn leaves in full leaf and the chestnut trees beginning to turn gold. Is it a warm fall day, or is the wind a little

109

sharp so that they huddle in their garments? Feel the wind, see the leaves shimmer, listen to the skitter of the leaves as they race along the ground. Imagine yourself walking among them and hear them crackle as you scuff your feet along, then feel them crumble to small pieces between your fingers. Their time has come and in a few weeks they will dissolve into the earth to be formulated into something else. This is also your Tide of Formulation, think about it. What choices are you making?

Blue, the color of balance and truth coupled with the circle brings imaginative ideas, thinking and reason. What are your beliefs now since you have come this far along the spiritual Path? Visualize your Angels on a mountain top or a windswept hill, they enjoy the airy feeling and the cleansing of the wind. Listen to their whispers, answer their questions. Have you decided what plans you are going to make during this Tide of Formulation? What changes would you like to see? This element of Air is extremely creative. Let your mind soar with ideas which you've never really entertained before, then later, see what remains behind after the Tide of Destruction passes through – you may be very surprised.

Once you have some idea of your future plans, you might consider activating them by putting the red fire triangle within the blue circle, giving you a double meaning. This will move things along for you with some interesting results. As you visualize the two colors together you may see a trace of a violet or purple color. Open yourself to receive feelings of nostalgia of your world before this incarnation, then feel yourself being filled with spiritual power.

Another interesting experiment with this blue circle is to visualize a number of circles put together. Then allow the circles to become spirals and within the spirals lies the sleeping serpent, the Kundalini, the symbol of wisdom, eternity and inner unity. This is another way to arouse the serpent, and if you are ready to handle its power you can activate it with this symbol. But be careful, it really is powerful.

With our final move into the winter Solstice comes the end of the year where you can look back at your achievements and you will also experience the death of some of your dreams. Angel Cetari guides in the Solstice and Sochiel encourages the earth to take a rest before its new work begins with the Vernal Equinox. Yellow is their color and the square is their symbol representing the material world of the four elements.

There's no duality here. The square represents stability, organization and construction. None of your airy, fairy dreams and "I wish", which haven't a chance of becoming anything worthwhile. These Angels will put you straight, in the nicest fashion, of course, and they will suggest that you meditate on a spiral within your yellow square which will give greater definition to the formulization of your previous plans.

Visualize them in their yellow garments, perhaps with a touch of brown in the trimmings to remind you that the dead and worthless are no longer extant. They deal with matter, reason, adaptation and orderly arrangement, so ask them what they have for you. As you make contact with them, try to smell the sharpness of winter in the air, feel the solidity of the earth beneath your feet, see the clarity of the sky heralding a cold night, or the heaviness of the clouds holding snow. The snow clouds can suggest to you a way to melt your difficulties and as it crystallizes again, so an idea or project can come in a flash of illumination. Visualize your own winter scene. Look at the bare trees covered with a light dusting of snow. See the woodland branches drooping down with their burden of snow. Smell the wood smoke in the air and visualize the winter warmth inside the houses. Hurry through the woods to meet your Angels who are waiting for you outside their own winter home. They will greet you and usher you inside the warmth, seating you comfortably so your discussions can begin. This Tattvic symbol opens a door between the two states of being. A new spiritual phase is opening up and also (as above, so below again), a new phase of life and opportunities are coming up for you. There will be decisions you have to make. This is the time to consult with these two Angels who will give you all the help you need.

Although this yellow square represents firmness and stability, if you visualize it standing on one of its corners, it changes its shape into a diamond, thereby changing its basic symbolism. A dynamic sense is brought into play. Desires of the material kind can be sought after, if this is your need or requirement. But you can also go after intellectual and spiritual knowledge, because the yellow square brings Spirit into matter.

If you put the red triangle into the yellow square, again you are changing its symbolism. Do you recall we talked about numbers way back in chapter 2? The triangle represents number three and the four points of the square added to the three brings the number seven into being. Remember we said the number seven was important? So using these two symbols together tends to bring all things into being, and due to the occult virtues of the seven, change will most definitely take place.

The last symbol you can use to make changes in your spiritual and material worlds is the oval: sometimes called the Black Egg or Indigo, if you feel you cannot visualize black. This is also occasionally referred to as the Babe in the Egg of Blue; the unconscious wisdom within the hidden source. We mentioned this oval once before when we talked about the silver crescent, so you should be able to visualize its shape. This energy is not easy to touch and you may have to work a long time to reach even a minutest flash, for this is creation in its purest form.

Its two most essential aspects are its own energy coupled with our material earthly form expressed by the four symbols we have just described above which are representative of the four worlds we talked about earlier in chapter 2: the earth plane (the square), the formless mass of the mental plane (the circle), the constructive materialized energy of the creative plane (the squared spiral), and the cosmic energy of power of the archetypal plane (the circles which became spirals); leading us into the cosmic egg which is the point we have now reached in our search for Divinity and the Oneness. Everything you have read and worked on in the previous chapters is now coming together. You will notice that bit by bit each chapter has led into the next one; joining up the energy patterns to eventually become a wholeness of self.

Should you propel the energy of the Egg into action, again moving the Kundalini upwards, activating and lighting up all your Chakras, you will experience both creativity and destructiveness taking place at the same time. Are you really ready for this? Consider carefully before moving into this meditation.

The whirlwind or hurricane type force which will whip through you will destroy what you think to be the most cherished material wholeness of yourself. Whatever you consider yourself to be at this time will no longer be. What is destroyed will be replaced by creative light, fulfillness and progressive development.

Within this chapter, you have been given the activity and dynamism of pure spirit with which to work, balanced by material things: the four elements, the four seasons, the four cardinal points and the four stages of life which bring order and stability into our world in which we create our own reality. Bear in mind that these Tattvic symbols can be used any time you feel yourself at a low ebb. Make your choice of symbol, for these symbols open the gates of the body and mind. And when you have completed your session, both your psyche and your physical body will feel thoroughly refreshed and full of vitality.

Chapter 9
Cause and Effect
What is Karma?

eality – what is it and how do we make it? In a nutshell, reality is what we think we see, feel and experience. It's our own particular happening or circumstance. It's what we consider exists within our own little microcosm, and how we respond to it. This microcosm is our own small world inside ourselves with which we align our own truths and beliefs of the moment.

How do we make this reality? We're back again to thought power and reactions as we mentioned in previous chapters. Thought can be an idea (in a positive and creative sense), or it can be a negative response to an unwanted or unpleasant situation. Either way, your thought equals connections (your reaction) to what has just taken place, upon which you are faced with choices. Now you have to make decisions about those choices, which then produces action, and there you have the consequences which finally translate into cause and effect. And cause and effect is what? Just plain old Karma as we mentioned in chapter 1. Just as you selected your own experiences before you were born, so you continue to create your own reality through your choices, decisions and how you respond to what you have chosen. As we've pointed out before, our minds are unconsciously painting pictures, or forming the environment through our thoughts which constantly change it – hence the importance of the development of mind control. If you have negative thoughts and beliefs, they'll float to the top causing disruption within your self and your surroundings. And if you really believe in evil, you'll create your own demons and experience them, because they are in your mind as part of yourself. To counterbalance, send out shining thoughts instead and remember you are made up of the values in which you believe, which forms your reality.

This reality business and its karmic results is actually most intriguing when you delve into it. One produces the other and vice versa and past, present and future each have their own past, present and future. How? Well, you had a karmic debt from your past which you wanted to clear off your slate by reincarnating into this earth plane. So you chose your experiences and your parents who would provide the necessary environment for this time around. This was your chosen future. Upon arrival in this world, your planned future now became your present.

The future that you planned for yourself was all very clear to you before you reincarnated because, within the Planes, you can see the effect of an action (the end product) before the cause (the stimulus) which prompted you to take that action. As time does not exist within the Planes (it's a man-made commodity), you can see the future you have just created and also the past and the present because everything exists as one. It has been, it is and it will be, but what there is, is molded and changed by thought power and visualization. Now, there's an enigma for you!

So in effect, before you reincarnated, you were able to sort things around, select these or those experiences and weave them together into a pattern until you were satisfied with the web you created. Then that future was laid out before you and you could see how it would all play out. But, once you got here (remember you drank of the waters of forgetfulness?), you forgot how you planned to eliminate that karma. Now, it's in your past.

Having arrived here in your new incarnation, you are now in your present reality. As you progress with your life, what you did with the early part, how you handled situations, people and your environment, which we talked about before, laid the foundation for your future. As you approached that future, your present fell into the past leaving you with a different reality that you created for yourself, removing that previously built future also into a past because you unwittingly changed it. Now you have restructured a new present, new future and another reality which you have built from your own daily responses.

So what we have here it would seem, is the uncertainty principle; not being able to predict exactly what will take place in the future because you have forgotten what you originally planned. So it's not really surprising that you have many different experiences from the ones you expected. Two of our inner Planes group who are on the other side (that we mentioned in chapter six), related their experience to us which had surprised them, and us in the telling, which gave us further insight into the Planes.

The boys, as we called them, would each take turn in speaking through Geof (recall we mentioned earlier that Geof developed into a trance medium, they are called channelers now). We used to have a session on Sunday evenings. It was Ptanu's evening to bring us insights from the other side and, during the course of the evening, he announced that he was reincarnating and saying his goodbyes to us. He told us he had chosen a Brazilian family of some wealth and was going to become an architect. He described to us some of the buildings he was going to design, and it seemed he would eventually become well known. We said goodbye knowing he would rejoin the group again when his earthly time was over, but you can imagine our surprise a few years later when he popped in again one Sunday evening. His whole life which he had planned so carefully came to a sudden end when a building he was passing was blown up and he went with it. He said he was greatly surprised to find himself back with the group. He had been in the wrong place at the wrong time, because he had decided to take the long way around and window shop while he carried out an errand for his parents. Ptanu's choice on that day altered the shape of his path of destiny and his Karmic path.

An even more intriguing story involves 'Arry (he never pronounces the aitch), and many people who read this book will remember having listened to him and spoken with him on Sunday evenings when he was speaking through Geof. He didn't tell us he was reincarnating and it was some time before I realized he hadn't been around. One Sunday evening when Timothy came through Geof, I remembered to ask and was told 'Arry had already gone on his way some time back and reincarnated into an army family. His new father was a Colonel and they had named him the impossible name of Ethel red (calling him Red for short), which amused the boys considerably. One Sunday evening about five years later, 'Arry's voice said to me "ullo, 'ere I am then." 'Arry went on to tell me that he didn't like the family he had chosen. He didn't fit he said, and he didn't like the discipline his army father imposed on him, so he changed places with Timothy who found it was exactly the environment he needed to fulfill his requirements. Timothy, in his previous life, had wanted to be a concert pianist, but he had been called up for service in World War II, captured by the Germans, used for some nasty experiments, managed to escape, was recaptured and was finally shot. Here was a golden opportunity for him to be part of a family in which discipline was required for his music. Timothy also retained some knowledge of his previous army discipline. 'Arry tells me he's doing extremely well, enjoying his life and is now writing his own music and performing at concerts. So what was it that 'Arry and Timothy exchanged? 'Arry says it was their consciousnesses (souls) that made the trade. The actual name for this is metempsychosis, meaning a transmigration of souls from body to body. We didn't know that this was possible, and it opened our eyes to further workings within the Inner Planes. Didn't somebody say "there are more things in Heaven and Earth?"

So here we are again back to the uncertainty principle and it would appear that the actions we take shape our lifetime. In Ptanu's case, his thought of window shopping (his choice) became his decision, altering the warp and woof of the fabric of his bit of the Universe. The consequence of his action changed his whole Karmic path and actually paid off some of his Karma. A case of win some (paying off Karma) and lose some (missing out on wealth and fame). The Universe is very fair.

Karma is an interesting subject to think about, especially when you consider that there is more than this one personal karma which we have been discussing. There is World karma. Every soul gets a bit of this; geographic Karma, the Karma of an area; racial karma of a tribe of people, and they all interlock in one way or another, eventually affecting your own personal Karma.

So what is World Karma and where did it come from in the first place? We did a lot of research throughout a variety of religions; the Greek and Hindu philosophy systems; Buddhism, Shintoism, Taoism. We searched the Upanishads, the Bhagavad Gita and a load more stuff, but nowhere could we find even a minor lead. Finally we came up with our own theory.

Imagine now, within this Universal Mind is a consciousness contemplating Its surroundings. For a long while, It absorbs the Nothingness which envelops It until It reaches a point of loneliness and suffocation. It says to itself, "This Nothingness is claustrophobic, it's too loving, too peaceful. It's simply a Oneness that does nothing for itself – or for me. We are unbalanced and we need some shadow to go along with this light, some opposition so that we may grow and develop an awareness. How can the consciousness that **I AM** build up energy patterns which will motivate this Mind to expand itself?"

Seating **Itself** in a comfortable armchair amidst the swirling Nothingness of love, peace, harmony and light, it gradually dropped into a dream state where mind pictures began to take shape.

Over the eons, consciousness watched **Its** thoughtforms take shape. Out of **Its** dream mists, first came the intelligences of the four elements: earth, air, fire and water. Out of the energy patterns of the elements appeared the gods, then appeared he who holds up the world. "I shall divide this Nothingness into useful spaces," he announced. "We shall have continents, islands, deserts and woodlands, water and air in abundance and mountains on which we Immortals shall live, and I shall be called Atlas." And live they did. Spreading themselves among the various geographic areas that Atlas had put together, the gods brought the balance into being within Universal Mind. They laughed and played, loved and hated, and when things weren't going their way, they were jealous and spiteful. They practiced a bit of incest here and there, then chopped up the babies in case they grew up and usurped their positions. They basked in peace and joy, then strife and conflict would take place. They kidnaped, then killed and renewed each other, fought over the craziest things and tried to outdo one another with their conquests. What marvelous cause and effect they were unwittingly brewing.

Despite their emotional reaction to each other, the gods were very intelligent and creative. They invented musical instruments, shared music, dance and poetry amongst themselves. Hermes, the god of thieves, invented the lyre. Pan made his pipe of seven reeds which he named Syrinx. The nine muses produced epic poetry, love poetry, lyric poetry, sacred poetry, tragedy and comedy, choral song and dance, also history and astronomy. Thoth taught wisdom to all of them, plus the system of hieroglyphics which eventually led to writing. Asclepius taught healing. Apollo also taught healing, along with music and

120

archery. Chiron taught medicine, and hunting with horses provided by ill-tempered Poseidon who caused earthquakes when he got into one of his snits.

Dionysus went one better than any of the others. He invented wine and introduced the vine into many lands. He was followed around by a crowd of frenzied women and this handsome, powerful god spent his time in drunkenness, debauchery and licentiousness of all kinds. Despite Dionysus' orgiastic rites, drama (especially tragedy) developed out of the traditional ceremonies performed at Dionysian festivals which in turn eventually influenced the philosophies and writings of Pindar, Plato, Pythagorus and Euripedes. Both sides of the balance again!

Gradually, within the timelessness of time the population of the gods increased. Although enjoying **Itself** enormously, watching their antics, the **I AM** consciousness decided that the knowledge the gods had developed should be shared with other energies. "What shall we do next?" **It** enquired of Atlas, who promptly sought out his father Iapetus, who had the answer to everything. And out of his thoughts, the human race was born.

And so we mortals grew, adoring and copying the movements of the gods, little knowing that the Fates were controlling our destinies, transferring their Karma to us. This was partly Poseidon's fault. Quarrelsome being that he was, he didn't have much love for the gods. He was on the side of the mortals, so he stole the sacred fire from Hestia, the custodian. In showing them how to use it, he educated humanity and illuminated their minds with the knowledge of flame which they used to keep warm and to learn to cook food. Now that the mortals no longer needed to eat only herbs and berries, they learned how to grow, harvest and cook grains and crops. Knowledge was born, they discovered how to make implements to kill animals, technical advances took

121

place and that's how world Karma got dumped on our shoulders.

Being so close to the gods in those early days, mortals listened to their whispered tales of everything that had happened to them. They modeled themselves on their precious gods despite their outrageous behavior(and we haven't changed much, have we?)

As we gradually evolved, moving back from our celestial gods, we became less spiritual and more material and the energy of the gods receded. The growth of souls was gradually taking place. People moved restlessly from place to place inflicting their desires, their greed, hatred, jealousy and pride on each other causing wars, just as their gods had in previous times. Geographic Karma was taking place and the spirit of negativity was sown in the ground to remain and expand as long as mortals continued to live in their ignorance.

This ignorance of the Oneness moved on into hatred of skin color and a variety of religious beliefs which vied with each other, for they couldn't live without a god of some description. Then, levels of greatness on the totem pole took place and people were segregated into subordinate positions; slaves who were treated badly, dragged into captivity or driven from their regions, wandering sadly from pillar to post only to receive the same treatment no matter where they went. Thus Racial Karma began and still continues at a rolling pace.

The gods looked on in horror at what was developing within the human race and decided amongst themselves that mortals needed guidance and some sort of protection. The intelligences of the four elements seemed to be hanging around not doing very much so they offered them the job of being the guardians of mortal souls and gave them the name of Angels.

And **It**, who is the Oneness, the **I AM** consciousness nods approval and sits within Universal Mind fully conscious of what has been, what is, and what is to come. For as far as **It** is concerned, everything has already happened and had before **It** sat down to contemplate.

Chapter 10
The Creative Plane and the Museum of Time and Space

So how much Karma do you have left? Perhaps you can discover that as you travel into this Creative Plane. But the creativity here is two fold. It deals with your creative self which is important to your well-being, and also with the development of ideas which we mentioned in chapter 2. Later, perhaps you can take a Mind Walk to view the blueprints and new inventions which are being prepared for future use.

Before we start looking into your own creative transformation, we should ask if you've really done the exercises. No doubt you read through the book first, a sensible thing to do; then you would know what to expect when you started over again. This is not a "dipping " book, per se. For the best results, you should read the book first, then work through the exercises chapter by chapter. Later, whenever you need to work a chapter for a specific purpose, you can go directly to it because you already know how to prepare yourself in advance. You see, each chapter is designed to segue into the next, enlarging on that piece of information to give you greater clarification and insight. Theoretical knowledge really won't do you much good. It might be an interesting talking point amongst friends, but you won't find the enlightenment you are seeking on your journey towards the Oneness. This pathway is a guide for self knowledge, spiritual progress, learning how to become a better human being and quietly being an example for others to follow in your footsteps.

So before you step into the energy patterns of the Creative Plane, it requests that you do a personal "sweep and clean". This means you take a look back at yourself and view what inner transformation has taken place.

Who are you now? You are nothing like the person you were when you first started working with this book. Your ideas about yourself have totally changed and you see the material world from a different point of view; recognizing that the structure of our so-called world of reality is so impermanent. Change is happening all the time, not only to you but to everyone and everything around you because we are all connected. Nothing is separate. Science, in the shape of Quantum mechanics talks about everything being connected to everything else. It says there is no "me or "other" which is what metaphysics has been saying for centuries. Particles, galaxies, the matter from which we, ourselves, are made are totally inseparable and we all influence each other. With what? Our consciousness, and the projection of our thoughts. Way back in May 1971, Louis (one of our Inner Planes teachers) made a pointed remark to the class and here we quote his words : "For we are what we think – and although we are changing all the time, we are not the same people we were a year ago. Yet memory and visualization casts us back into the same old mold. The secret of shortening the Path is to cut off memory so that it does not chain us to what we were. For if we remain what we were, we must return to the physical Plane to become what we should be". That is the essence of chapter 4; making and understanding a profile of yourself, so you can cut off memory, become and keep on becoming that which you wish to become. The moment you think you have reached that pinnacle, you will find that you start all over again.

Having assiduously worked through all these exercises and taken firm control of your mind, your thoughts are now very powerful. They can bring into being what you have generated within your

126

mind – both positive and negative. Remember Glendower, Shakespear's character from the play Henry IV, who said, "I can call spirits from the vasty deep?" For you now, they will come. So be careful how you direct your thoughts. You can be a power house for changing the environment around you (in either direction). And the people who are close to you will follow your example; even though they may not consciously be aware of doing so.

We mentioned in earlier chapters that you would be constantly consulting your inner self and seeing the changes that have taken place within your self and your outer world. Keep making a record of your changes in your diary. In years to come when you look back at it, you will be amazed at what you have accomplished.

Having previously removed those recognized hang-ups, other stuff has probably floated to the top of your mind as you've examined yourself. What else do you need to get rid of? Now is a good time. We'll just mention here that you'll never completely get rid of the irritations, annoyances, quick rise of anger and other things the rest of the world trips us up with. The trick to overcoming these is not to let them remain within your mind. React to them if they really bug you, then let them traipse through one side and out the other, and then forget they even happened. Practice it, you'll get the hang of it and it will eventually become automatic. In the meantime, don't fret over your reaction.

Many years ago (July 12th 1971 to be exact), we were having the same trouble trying to ignore the nit-picking of students (and the friends they brought along for the Saturday evening gatherings). One evening was very frustrating and when they left, we consulted Louis, and this was his answer: "Reaction to people is the impurity which is the last to be eradicated. Resist the vibrations which reach you as best you may, and use them as a constructive test of the extent of spiritual harmony within". Louis knows what he was talking about. Before his death, he was a British World War I fighter pilot who was shot down by a German aviator in 1917 and burned to death in his plane. In some of our talks, he had mentioned that he was very patriotic then (he was only 16 when he joined the RFC, the Royal Flying Corps), angry at the German side who tried to take over his country. He took that anger into the air each time he had to fly and fight the enemy. When he was shot down, he took his anger to the other side with him, and also his hatred of the German who cut his life so short (he was less than 19 when he died). He said it took him a long time to work through it to get it out of his consciousness, which impeded his spiritual growth.

We don't need to take anything like that to the other side when we go. It delays our progress and is best dealt with here. His advice is very valuable and we should look at our own inner transformation in the here and now and make sure it stands up to the trials of our existence, as well as work on developing our inner peace. He also suggests that, "The further you can take your mind into the Inner Planes, so grows a modicum of peace and harmony and all the other positive attributes of existence on the earth plane."

Now, with this new power and vision you have developed, is it possible that you can set causes in motion within this Creative Plane? Indeed it is. Once again, we will reinforce what has been said before: if you can create the illusion of the world around you by the power of your belief of the moment and believe it is reality, you can instruct your mind to create whatever you want in the Inner Planes, and transformation will take place in your outer world. Your mind does not judge, it only recognizes what it is told and it simply does what it is told to do.

Any creation we make now taps into the alchemical secret of the Universe (naturally bringing about change), so it is most important that the will and intent be extremely focused. Recall the Know, Will, Dare and Keep Silent mentioned in Chapter 6? Develop a unique vision of your own, setting your goals within. Build yourself a mental bridge between this earth world and the true world of reality beyond, and you will find that you have also developed the perfect marriage between inspiration and the technique of expression.

Developing the strength and the use of the White Light as you have been shown before, and by using it with great focused ability, you can decrease the Uncertainty Principle to a great extent, because you are becoming in charge of your own destiny – up to a certain point. That point being called the Fork in the Road (we mentioned our own in chapter 8), a true destiny point where the decision you are about to make will change everything, including your Karma. At this time, your Angels will be of the greatest help in offering you guidance, but even they can be overruled by Higher-Ups depending on what these Higher Beings require from you. You'll recognize when you've reached one of these Forks, because it brings with it a dilemma – and believe us, the choice will be difficult.

There are three principle steps to be aware of when you reach this destiny point:
    1: the clarity of the situation,
    2: the use of logic instead of quick emotional decisions and
    3: the movement.

When you recognize what is happening, sit down and try to clarify the whole situation. What brought you to this point? What was the happening that caused it, or stimulated you to take the previous action? Look at the result. Are you satisfied or dissatisfied with the action you took to bring this result to you?

Now you have two or maybe even three different directions you can take, and you must analyze them carefully with every bit of logic you can muster before you take even one step. This is where your goal setting comes in. Think in images. Form strong pictures in your mind and use the symbols you were taught in the previous exercises. At this stage of your development, the energy patterns of the Beings can only recognize symbols, colors and the vibrations of music (which we'll talk about later).

When you have thought your goals through and balanced everything to your satisfaction, then, and only then, should you make the movement and put your decision into action. Once done, you are going to live with the results. Hopefully you will enjoy them.

Now I'd like you to stop here for the moment. Leave your images and goals to one side and we'll come back to them in a short while. I have a couple of little stories to share with you and you'll see how our minds can tune in to the Oneness of everything when it is totally relaxed and removed from the bonds of Earth. When you've read and enjoyed our experiences, we will return to your goals/plans and your visit to the Lords of Karma who will help you with your decision making to take you through your Fork in the Road.

This Creative Plane is a delightful place in which to spend time. Through your previous mental development, you should be able to clairvoyantly see the energy patterns of the deities which inhabit our earthly world. There really are fairies at the bottom of the garden. And having trained your mind to touch the reality of the other world, you should be able to catch a glimpse of the spirits, the muses, and everything else that lives in the rivers, mountains, streams, flowers, woodlands, stones, soil, anything you like to name.

Everything has its own consciousness which interacts with everything else. You probably know about or believe in Patron Saints who you can call on? When you do this, you are trying to touch the consciousness, the energy pattern of your belief. Think about this too; every endeavor you undertake has its own "patron spirit" with whom you can communicate and receive help. Trees, for instance, are full of energy. If you are feeling depleted, put your arms around a tree and absorb the energy it will give you. Or just sit under it and relax against it. Let your mind drift and see how you feel some time later. You'll be very surprised. I (Maiya) adore Willow trees and tuck myself beneath their weeping branches and rest against the trunk. Nobody knows I'm there, and I can spend time renewing myself spiritually and physically.

I had the most incredible experience one time when I was out painting a landscape. Out in the country, surrounded by trees, I'd stopped to view my work and to have a little rest on my stool. As I contemplated my painting and gazed at the trees, the light gradually began to change into a vibrating golden color. The trees seemed to take on a different dimension. Their branches reached out to enfold me and I was filled with an energy and love I had never encountered before in my earthly existence. Elms, evergreens, oaks, willows, all the varieties of this wonderful woodland showed me their auras and energy patterns and welcomed me into their fold. They whispered to me in their own way which I understood, and as I returned their love with the joy I felt, the whole woodland seemed to vibrate and echo with "come again, come again". Although I have absorbed the energy from many trees in other different places, I have never experienced anything like that again. Each time I sit under a tree I wait, will it happen again? Perhaps I try too hard and the frame of mind is not quite right – one day – one day.

131

Some years ago, a fellow Geof was working with was on his way home from work feeling quite worn out. Geof and Kevin both worked for a newspaper under a most trying boss, and Kevin decided to stop off at Lighthouse Park (a little park that not many people knew about). Relaxing on a bench under a tree and leaning into the trunk, Kevin said he couldn't believe his eyes when he saw a fairy. He thought at first he was dreaming, blinked, found himself wide awake and sat quietly watching this little Being at work. Its mouth was moving and he realized it was talking to the wild flowers it was moving amongst. He was so enchanted and watched for a long time. Then he accidentally moved on his bench and the fairy turned, waved and vanished from sight. He told Geof about this encounter only because, "You're in this funny business and you'd understand." Kevin said that later when he really thought through this experience, he found it had changed his life and understanding of the world around him.

When Geof was a young boy, around seven or eight, he used to see a little man sitting on the hood of his father's car. When they were traveling, he sometimes wondered why he didn't fall off or get blown away. Much later on, in the early 1960's when Geof was working for NASA in South Africa, he had to travel some forty miles home from the tracking station through the veldt. It was a long drive in the dark after a tiring three day shift and he often mentioned a protective spirit who used to sit in the passenger seat. Many years later we discovered it was Ptanu who used to accompany him.

Remember the garden Devas you saw on your first Mind Walk in chapter 6? With all the exercises and mind work you have done, you've finally broken the barriers between the worlds and now you should be able to see them and their friends very clearly. My Grandmother used to call them "the little people", and on warm quiet days, she and I would sit in the garden and watch them working and playing. Grandmother had a big bird bath which they

132

used as their own swimming pool. They'd play in it or sit around the rim exactly the way we would enjoy our own pool.

There was one special night which was absolutely captivating. Grandmother had invited me to spend the weekend and just before midnight she woke me, telling me to dress warmly and come quietly into the garden. We sat for quite some time and then they came. A huge gathering of fairies, nymphs, elves, pixies, leprechauns, animals and the music makers. Grandmother nudged me to be very quiet. It was a very special time she whispered, the ball was in honor of Queen Mab, the queen of the fairies. They had transformed the garden into their own little outdoor ballroom, putting fairy lights on the bushes and trees and the whole affair was incredibly enchanting. They danced and sang – their voices to our ears sounding like sweet toned bells. What marvelous colors scintillated from the lanterns hanging from the trees. Their fancy dresses and suits taking on different shades of color as they swirled the floor. When it was time for the musicians to take their break, jesters and jugglers took their turn. Leprechauns danced the Irish jig. Then some clever skits were performed mimicking the ego and density of humans bringing hoots of laughter and clapping from the onlookers.

We watched until it was nearly dawn then went back inside to bed. I remember lying there experiencing again what I had just witnessed, finally dropping off to sleep. Grandmother and I kept our wonderful secret to ourselves vowing to watch again the next year. Unfortunately, she wasn't around. She fell during the winter, broke her hip and never recovered. I never watched again.

There are so many other little sprites, garden devas, tree sprites, water nymphs and similar "little people" whose lives you can experience. Believe and they will come to you without any strain on your part; purely because we're all so much a part of each other.

Having digressed a little bit to show you how your mind has opened up to the hidden world around you, we hope you have now spent some time setting up your goals as previously suggested. Now, to go along with your goals/plans we'll mentally build a Star Wand, a Star of Fire; a powerful tool to use within this Plane to bring them into being. Remember we mentioned the six-pointed star in chapter 8? This wand is built from that symbol and represents the Will: the wisdom and spiritual presence of your creative self. Your desire to experience what lies within this Creative Plane, coupled with your imagination and charged by your magical Will, sets up a magnetic attraction in the Astral Light, and the Cosmic Gods will respond to this symbol. Recall what we said in Chapter 1 about force and form doing bidding? You need this form to bring this force into action. So any time you have a quiet moment to yourself, practice, practice and practice. Visualize a six-pointed star wand with flames pulsating through and around it. Just get the feel and sight of it until it seems to be so real that you could almost burn yourself on the flames. Don't activate it or your goals until you've gone into your Mind Walk which will come up next.

This chapter of exercises and workouts seems to be a bit back to front compared with other chapters, but it is essential to make these preparations of goals, plans and wand beforehand, as they will be activated at the end of your Mind Walk. They must be ready to set in motion. Move on now and you'll understand more later on.

At the beginning of this chapter, the question was "How much karma do you have left?" Now, the time has come for you to find out by visiting the Lords of Karma through your Mind Walk which is why your Fork in the Road decision is on hold for the moment. Within this Mind Walk, you can see how your Karma is shaping up, and also the effect of your goals/plans which will take place once you have set the cause in motion. Recall we said earlier that within the Planes you can see the effect before the cause? Point your mind in the right direction and you can see ahead what will happen once you set things in motion. Then you can make your decision as to whether you wish to continue with the choice you've made, or back off and rethink.

When looking at or discussing your Karmic debt with the Lords of Karma, consider your emotional reaction. Is there a quandary? If so, think again – carefully – about the plans or goals you have on hold. Not quite satisfied with them and the end result? Then plan something else.

Now here's another factor. Although you have chosen plans or goals which seem to be right for you, and the effect appears to be good in your earthly world, the Lords of Karma may well point out something you have missed and suggest you go a different route, choosing what you need (and can't see) over and above what you want. Pay heed to their advice, they could save you a lot of karmic debt, although the ultimate choice is yours.

When everything is acceptable to you and you have finished your discussion with the Lords of Karma, they will guide you as you put your wand and your plans into action. This requires just a slight mind movement and the Lords will step behind you while you take charge of your next step. Visualize your pulsing, vibrating, fiery star wand. Hold it in your hand as you tell yourself that you are now putting your plans and goals and anything else you have chosen into action. Concentrate completely on what is happening, because visualization and willpower must work together. Lose yourself entirely in this sensation. Feel the swell of the energy pattern as movement within the warp and woof of the Universe takes place. You should feel as if you are in movement and being carried along. The Lords of Karma are behind this as they mentally roll this causal energy into place, steadying for a time, the uncertainty principle that surrounds you.

Now you know what to expect and what lies ahead, so get ready for your Mind Walk. Prepare yourself as before with the relaxation and the White Light which should now be so automatic that it happens very quickly. Mentally walk up the Path, open the gate (of the mind), grab your Angels and away you go to the Creative Plane. Your Angels enjoy this Plane enormously because of the beauty and the interacting love vibrations that surround everything and every Being. They feel fulfilled and renewed each time they visit this Plane.

Your first introduction here is to the Angel Uretil, Scribe of the Most High. He is expecting you. Your own Angels will wander off on their own business and Angel Uretil will converse with you before ushering you into the presence of the Lords of Karma. You will then continue on as outlined previously – discussing first your goals and plans with them, listening to their advice. They will direct you when it is time to put your wand and plans into action. Remember to visualize strongly and the Lords will add their power along with yours.

Here we have to leave you for we do not know what you will see or hear regarding your own Karma, or what you will talk over with the Lords of Karma. This is all very private, between yourself and the four Lords (you will meet the other seven later). The only other Being who knows what is going on is the Angel Uretil, the keeper of the books and records who will record everything in his book. The moving finger writes and having writ moves on! And so will you, cherishing an experience that no words can describe.

We (Geof and I) are also moving along. If you recall, in chapter 8, we mentioned that we had reached a Fork in the Road in our destiny; waiting to see the next step. Many of you will be wondering what happened to us as we reached our crisis point. Here's the result.

Utilizing the advice we gave to you earlier in this chapter, we followed those three steps of clarifying our situation, applying logic, and then making the movement after looking at the effect we would produce. First, we took time out to visit another province after looking at houses on the Internet. The prices were very acceptable (cheaper than in our own province where prices were rising rapidly). Then we selected a number of houses which appealed to us and away we went.

Driving from town to town, we viewed them, thought about them, and turned them all down until we came to the last house on our list. There it was in all its majesty. A beautiful one hundred year old house, empty for two years (except for a couple of ghosts), so we were able to bargain for it. With the cash we had received from the sale of the previous house (our harvest), we were able to purchase it without need of a mortgage (a desire we had placed in the Spiritual Planes a couple of years back). So you see, things do finally drop into place with satisfaction all around. There is a health care center close by for Geof and a retinal surgeon not too far away. Unfortunately, he had to have a second operation on his eye, so he needs further care.

As I write now, the Vernal Equinox has just moved in. Change is taking place for us and we move into our new province in a couple of months putting into action our plans that survived the Tide of Destruction. Interesting how things work out, huh?

We said a little way back that this Creative Plane is a most interesting place to visit. Indeed it is, for here, with just another little mind twitch, instead of being in the Lords of Karma's space, you can take a visit to the Museum of Time and Space.

We'd like to mention here that all these levels and Planes we have been discussing are really all in one place. They co-exist, and they are all in the same place at the same time just as sound, light and heat may exist in the same place without mutual interference. It has been necessary to use the terms "levels and the next Plane" until now because the Western world has a habit of putting things in boxes and labeling them. The Western mind, when encountering something new or different, expects to be guided in steps, which tends to restrict the development and expansion of thinking patterns and awareness. It's odd really when you consider the total acceptance of sound, heat and light existing together, and there is no quibble about that. Yet trying to get that same concept of the Planes all being in the same place into the minds of students presents a challenge, particularly when we say it takes just a little twitch of the mind and you'll find yourself in a different mental space.

Plato said, "Everything in the world is just the shadow of the real thing we can't see." But you, having reached this stage of acceptance, understanding and experience have learned that your lives really begin when you step across the borders from this world into the others. Where you really can "see" with your inner mind. The mind trips taken earlier were to hone your inner senses which are very much sharper than your outer senses. With this next Mind Walk into the Museum, you can reach into many other realms of existence recognizing that they do indeed exist all in the same place. It's a case of taking your mind into the area of your choice and walking through a time portal. Sound fascinating? Then let's go.

We don't really need to tell you how to get into your mind space now as you've done it so often, but to jog your memory: relax, breathe, bring down the White Light, walk down the path with your Angels, then through the gate (opening your senses) and arrive at the entrance to the museum.

Before you get started, entrance to the museum can only be achieved by programming your mind first – the area of your choice as we mentioned above. Unlike other Planes in which much of what you have encountered before is a fixture built by the minds of previous Chelas (mentioned in chapter 3), the museum doesn't exist until you want to visit it, it being part of the warp and woof – the web of the Universe. Just as all the levels and Planes we have described before, they too are part of the same web, all existing in the same place. But they were somewhat easier to achieve. Now, having moved into a finer stream of consciousness (you've disposed of a lot of your earthly baggage), you will have to program your mind first each time you take a Mind Walk. You are beginning to reach out for higher dimensions which only trained minds can touch.

You've programmed your mind now to arrive at the doors of the museum. You've called on your Angels, opened the gate of your mind and walked down the path. How you see the museum will be the choice of your imagination, just as you used it to build your portraits in chapter 3. Is it an old prestigious building whose beauty impresses you? Is it one of the modern buildings, all angles and pointed roofs? Is it made of glass and spires which gleam gold and flame when the sun strikes it? What do you feel when you gaze at it? Do you feel warmth inviting you in to satisfy your curiosity? Do you expect intellectual stimuli? Are you excited not knowing what to expect? Study and reserve your reactions as you will need them shortly. Whatever you experience, press the bell on the door and wait for it to open. Step inside and wait. Eventually, you will be greeted by the museum keeper. Once again, whatever you expect to see in the shape, size, coloring, etcetera of the keeper (your mind will paint the portrait), will be standing before you – welcoming you into his archives. To your total shock, you will discover as you look around that there is nothing there. There will be nothing there until you request whatever it is you wish to see and experience. The museum keeper will ask you which period of so-called time you wish to see – which Time Portal you wish to step into. Your choice entirely. You have the whole of history to choose from. As far back or as near as you wish, you may also visit the future. If you wish, you can choose to visit an alternative universe where the same developments of earth have taken place (i.e. planes, cars, TVs, computers, etc.). Not necessarily at the same time as we know of time, but earlier or later than our developments. You will see that other uses have been made of the technology they have discovered to which they have given different names. For instance, we had a world war using our planes and submarines. They avoided war which was totally unacceptable to them, but they use their planes purely for commerce and passenger flights and their submarines are underwater educational devices.

Be prepared to experience your choice on all levels of being – this is what your previous mind exercises were training you for. All your senses will be heightened and activated. You will be there, just as if you were experiencing a happening in your own earthly world. If you have chosen a violent period of history, you will find yourself clothed in that time period, perhaps riding a horse, brandishing a sword, charging forward for a kill. If you have chosen an archeological expedition for the time when the pyramids were first discovered, you will experience all the details there. If you choose the future, you may experience moving sidewalks which people step on and off at certain points. Perhaps you will see the many air terminals in town where people take air traffic instead of our transit system. Perhaps time machines and the Siwash drive will be available in the time period you have chosen. There's a whole load of fascinating time to choose from. Whatever you fancy, be aware you will feel everything with all your senses from fear right through to ecstasy. Make your choice wisely, but be aware that your Angel energies will accompany you as guides and protectors.

When you've made your decision, inform the museum keeper who will then explain to you that he will activate a Time Portal of the period you have requested. As the portal opens you will see a moving hologram into which you are expected to step. This time portal is what is known as the Akasha – a stream of Cosmic Light – onto which everything has been recorded – past, present and future. And the holograms themselves are reflections of this Cosmic Light.

As Mr. Spock (from that old TV series Star Trek) would say, "Fascinating." It certainly is, and in this museum, you really should spend a while exploring. And the more you explore, the more you'll discover within the Cosmic Light. On other visits to the museum, do ask the keeper to move your consciousness into alternative universes so you may experience how some of the creative stuff we talked about in earlier chapters has been used in different fashions, thereby changing their personal and world Karma.

Right now, your next adventure in consciousness is a visit to the Archetypal Plane and being introduced to the Angels of the Outer Planets, then a meeting with the Archangels. Ready? Then let's move right along.

Chapter 11

The Archetypal Plane, the Angels of the Outer Planets and the Archangels

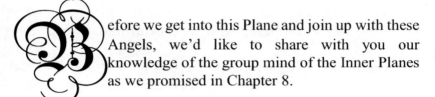efore we get into this Plane and join up with these Angels, we'd like to share with you our knowledge of the group mind of the Inner Planes as we promised in Chapter 8.

If you've always had an interest in occult/hidden things, you have probably been a member of your own group for a great length of time, possibly eons, but you haven't been aware of it. Perhaps in your dream time when you were younger, you've dreamt unusual things/meetings with people, but shrugged them off being unaware of your group connection. Naturally, as you got older and became involved in your material existence, the nightly visits became less and less. Then as you moved into your teens and full involvement with the world, your dream world changed and you no longer visited your group in that particular self. Now, as you pick up the Path again, you will become aware of your group association and start remembering the ties between all of you. You can put all these previous dreams together, recognize your group and get to know the work you do within the Inner Planes. You will also find that the rest of your group are people you have had many experiences with in your past lives over the centuries. They are no strangers to you. We are not talking Angels here. We are talking about real people who also have had many lives, have passed on to the other side and are now soul energy patterns. You will recognize them as they were the last time you saw them in the flesh – whenever that may have been.

Now, we do not know what your group or other groups are like, we only know they do exist. Each summer solstice, a chosen group puts on a pageant which lasts until the next summer solstice and all soul energies are encouraged to visit. We have (all of our group) experienced the soul energies of different groups within these pageants, so we do know they have a reality. Our own pageant on a Greek theme took place in 2002, and many different energies (including those from alternative universes) passed through. From these pageants we all learn something new.

Whether you are in a physical body or a spirit body, we all have work to do within the Planes. So don't think for one moment that when you get to the other side, you're going to take it easy, sitting on a cloud, singing all day! We've each got our chosen work to do; whatever we would like to do, whatever we feel we do well and enjoy doing. You may even have a special talent that you use in your sleep state that you are not aware of in your waking state. It may well materialize in this plane of reality once you become aware of the use of your inner and outer senses. When you sharpen the inner, the outer will pick up the knowledge and put it to use. Do you teach in the Planes? You know more than you think you do. Are you scientifically inclined? Do you wish to do healing? That's a fascinating area, nothing like the healing in this physical world. You are dealing with soul healing in the Inner Planes, not physical bodies. The healing there can be brought through into a physical body through the use of the White Light and/or the Chakras as we mentioned before.

There is also a very special type of healing in the Planes carried out in Spiritual Shrines. This is where the "sick" Angels and spirit bodies recuperate when they encounter certain situations, or have been drained by webs of negative energies which do exist within the Planes. The spirit healers get drained when they have been called to aid in the healing of souls when earthquakes, floods, hurricanes, tornadoes or terrorist attacks have taken place, and the souls come over in the thousands. The immensity of the trauma touches their emotions (which you take with you when you die) which starts to drain them, just as our hospital workers are drained when they react in the same way to these events. Now, you may be one of the physical (earth) people who have a certain energy pattern which becomes a "dynamo" for Inner Planes workers to draw on when they get into this negative energy state.

If you are one of these people, you will experience at times a mental, even physical lack of vital energy. You may have already had these experiences and wondered why you felt so worn out. Rest easy when it happens, treasure the knowledge. For you are doing very important work which the Inner Planes cannot do without. In fact, you are very privileged. This is probably the only work you'll be allowed to do within the Planes and your group. Dynamos are very necessary and well cherished in many ways for they have a particular and unusual energy pattern which only a few souls have.

One further specialized type of work carried out among certain groups of people is called a Rescue Circle which is done on this mundane Plane. As the name suggests, it is the rescue of trapped souls who enter and speak through a group of trance mediums who get together at specific times. (Ours used to meet once a week). This requires a group of fully developed trance mediums, two other people who act as "pillars" (not mediums). The energy patterns flow through these "pillars" to the leader of the group, who moves around speaking to each spirit within each medium.

The leader greets the spirit, then the spirit gives information of who he or she is. Then the leader explains to the spirit what is happening. Some of them do not quite realize they are dead. Some are still experiencing their trauma and need great comfort, but they will be told how they will be helped as they move on out. Very often, relatives are summoned by someone on the other side to give help to the soul. There is always a receiver spirit waiting for this new soul – one of your own Inner planes group whom you know will act as receiver – and the soul will be guided to its own place or group.

'Arry used to be our receiver. Lt. Timothy Jenkins (we mentioned earlier) and, our Doctor, Paddy O'Grady, both came through our rescue circle. I believe Bilious did too, but it's so long ago, I really can't remember. And so many, many more have been rescued during those years. The one case I do remember clearly which made me cry, was a fellow called Taffy. A Welsh miner, he had been trapped by a mine explosion some many years before he came to rescue, and he still didn't realize he was dead. Coming through our rescue circle, he was experiencing being rescued from the mine and being taken to hospital. His main concern and major request was that I get in touch with his wife. "Please tell her," he said, "that I will be late for breakfast." Through my tears, I called for 'Arry to take him and guide him on his way. Even now as I write, though this happened forty years ago, I still feel the tears welling up inside me for the love and concern Taffy had for his wife despite his own pain and injuries. More than likely, they are together again.

There are very few rescue circles left now, but if you can do this very necessary work in this Plane of ours, you'll find it both heart-breaking and rewarding in helping trapped spirits on their way to joy and happiness.

Getting back to other group work, within our group we have two healers. Dr. Paddy O'Grady, a genuine doctor in his previous life sometime in the mid 1800s, he was well versed in herbal treatments. He has just devised a method of bending, stretching and relaxing which, he informs us, is working very well for his patients in both the Inner and outer (our)Planes. His healing gets through to us in our sleep state, and he's certainly helped my hip which was damaged some years ago in an accident. We were also quite curious about what happens to the thousands of souls who suddenly arrive on the other side through accidents, bombings like the twin towers or the tsunami in Asia on December 28th of 2004. There are so many, many souls and we wondered how they received the help they needed.

Remember, we mentioned that everything in the Planes is created by thought? Paddy and all his helpers created a warm pool (rather like a huge swimming pool), and as the souls reached them, they took this conscious energy and floated it in the pool of warmth, love and care, and the soul healing started to take place.

Our second healer is 'Arry Plater (mentioned before), and many who already have met and spoken with him will be surprised. In his previous life during the 1930's, 40's and until his death in the early 50's, he was a thief and a pickpocket, known as 'Arry the Dip. He fell off a roof trying to avoid capture by the police and broke his neck. He's obviously mended his ways (and his neck), got interested in psychology (probably an interest from one of his past lives), and has chosen to take care of the healing of souls who were murderers, psychopaths; those who would be termed "dangerous inmates". They have a special area in which they are placed until they are healed and ready to move on. 'Arry says he enjoys his work very much. It's rewarding to see souls responding to his treatment.

We mentioned previously army lieutenant Timothy Jenkins. Although he has now incarnated again, he appears in our group in his sleep state occasionally and will join us again after his next death. We also have Darius who has been within the Planes for the last 4000 years having completed his time on earth, and Peter who has also been there for about 2000 or more years. Both Louis and myself were with Peter and Darius some millennia ago. Ptanu, we also mentioned earlier, is still teaching. Bilious, another of our group, is very busy these days. Why is he called Bilious? That's what we asked him many years ago when he used to speak through Geof doing past lives for people. He said he was named William, frequently called Bill, and when he was at school a new boy arrived who he befriended. "What's your name?" he asked, the newcomer replied "Julius, what's yours?" Not to be outdone, William replied "Bilious" and he's remained Bilious ever since. Bilious and I were of the same family way back in the 1400's. Anyway, he has a most interesting job. He's mapping the Ley Lines of the earth. These are the spiritual connecting lines around the globe. Eventually, a spiritual Chela will mentally pick up the idea, draw the map and build a spiritual temple in his/her area of choice. He/she will be guided and directed to choose the most potent place. By the way, Bilious tells us our house, (our new residence) is on a line with the Ley Line of Glastonbury Tor, in England. No wonder it's so peaceful.

Finally, Louis Hellerman, our World War One pilot, also mentioned earlier. He's my twin soul, once we were an amoeba, grew our souls, then we split. Since then, we've experienced many, many lives, sometimes together, sometimes apart. But our souls have finally joined together again. Geof, on the other hand is my soul mate. He appeared on the scene thousands of years ago and the three of us have had a love triangle going since then. Somehow or another Geof has been responsible so many times for Louis' death. The last time was during World War One when Geof was a German fighter pilot and shot him down causing Louis' painful death by burning. Finally, the antagonism between the two of them is over, they have accepted each other's energy patterns.

Louis also teaches in the Inner planes which he does extremely well. Before his death, when he was on this earth plane, he intended to become a car designer. Cars were the new thing at that time (he was born in 1898), and he's taken that desire with him. Instead of cars, he's designed and is building a time machine from the blue prints he found in the future, which, he says will be ready in the next century. When you take your mind walk into this Archetypal Plane, ask to see it. He'll be delighted to show it to you.

We've gone into all this detail of the people within our group to show you some of what goes on within the group minds of the Inner Planes, and how the people within our group and ourselves have been connected in previous lives. We hope you found it fascinating, because somewhere "out there", you also have a fascinating group of your own.

Next, we will talk about the Angels of the Outer Planets and how the planets are affecting you now. Then we'll show you how to make preparation for meeting the energies of the Archangels.

The energies of the outer planets work in two ways. These planets are Uranus, Neptune and Pluto and if you are into astrology, you will know a great deal about them. We can probably safely say, that if you have reached this far into the book, you've already investigated and worked with other disciplines of the mystical world such as palmistry, numerology, tarot cards, cabala and more. You will know that all these energy patterns are one and the same. How they are used depends on the individual.

In one of our teaching sessions – looking for a little proof – we did an astrology chart of a student, somebody else did a palmistry reading of the same student, another person did her numerology and then her tarot cards were read by a fourth person. An interesting feature was that all readings were almost identical in nature, astrology of course, being that much more detailed, but these disciplines do work together.

Getting back to these three planets, in the early years of life, they naturally govern more of the material world and for people who are not interested in other worldly things, they will continue to vibrate along earthly interests. For those of us who choose to follow the Path of Light, these vibrations develop a higher frequency. This is why you find yourself really plagued with Divine Discontent wanting to know more, and more and more. So by the time you've reached the age of 56, these planets have done a number of trips around your astrology chart and have joined up together to make a trio, all working together. If you have always had an interest in this sort of thing, then your own Angels and the Angels of the outer planets will bring you the opportunities to move onto the Path. If you have been walking the Path earlier, your intensity will be doubled.

At this time, Uranus is the higher and lower mind working as one. Saturn's higher vibration will also lend its influence to the sign Aquarius (the home of Uranus), but Saturn needs the vibrations of lofty Uranus for these two planets to work in tandem, bringing out Saturn's esoteric side.

When Uranus and Saturn are joined by the subtle and intangible influence of that beautiful, mystical planet Neptune, your spiritual consciousness is really awakened and the underlying cycles and rhythms of the Universe will impinge on your mind. Pluto will take you across the abyss bringing regeneration and transformation of self. Unless you've really done your exercises and trained your mind with the expectation of going beyond the Veil, these wonderful, uplifting vibrations may well go unnoticed and untouched. This would be a pity, because there are many fabulous experiences to come with the aid of the Angels of these three planets.

As you may have realized by now, all the Angel energies we've mentioned in chapter one (for all the signs) affect all people at different times of life. This vibrational state will impinge on all the people walking the Inner Paths, not just the signs they rule.

What to expect having reached this far in your spiritual disciplines? First off, that important Crown Chakra associated with spiritual awakening will bring on a jolt of Kundalini energy – and we really do mean a jolt. You'll feel it from the base of your spine traveling up to a hefty wallop at the back of your head. As we mentioned before, we are all made up of patterns of vibratory energy: light, sound and color. Some of you will develop the ability to see these rays of colored light around people and, perhaps even to hear their musical soul notes when you come in close contact with them.

What else will you find in these subtler realms of reality? You will meet many different spiritual teachers and you will witness the wave pattern with which they mentally communicate. You will see the most beautiful landscapes, mountains, trees, forests and lakes; far more scintillating than the ones you've experienced in earlier mind walks. You will also encounter spirits from other planets and dimensions.

Many Yogic practices teach how to reach these other planes of reality through a shift of consciousness, just as we have been teaching you in previous chapters. In fact, we have now passed on all the knowledge you need to access these various planes. We can only describe to you what we and others have experienced in our meditational and dream worlds. When you reach any of these realms, your thoughts will materialize anything you desire – a marvelous experience. The most striking thing about these worlds is the radiant vibrations of which everything is comprised, and the intensity of joy, love and delight of existence within these realms.

We could go on for many pages about the beauty of the inner worlds with their halls of learning which appear to be built out of knowledge; the libraries and seminar rooms, the luminous cities, all reachable by your journey into the hidden depths of your mind.

Here, we would like to mention that you have now reached the most difficult portion of this book and you should not expect immediate results. Contact here requires deep meditation, almost to the point of being in a trance-like state. So please don't be disappointed at the time it takes. The biggest battle is trying to silence the constant chatter of words and thoughts which keep traipsing through the mind. But to explore the depth of these planes of consciousness, you'll have to sharpen your powers of concentration. Keep practicing, it will happen when you least expect it.

How about those Archangels. Actually, there are seven. The well known ones being Raphael, Michael, Gabriel and Uriel. The other three go off to do their thing leaving the four to guard the four corners of the Universe. These Angels of course, are not the originals. They've long gone onto other things in higher planes, but as these Angels move on up, there are others to take their places utilizing the names people know them by. As we have said on a number of occasions, when you meet them, they will take on the shape and form appropriate to your mind set – your particular consciousness.

You'll enjoy these Angel energies. They are quite fun to meet. This particular batch of Archangels took over just a few thousand years ago and they have quite a sense of humor. When we say they will take on a form suitable for you, if they are in a playful mood, they may take on a shape that was last in your mind. Geof had the fortune to meet them a few weeks ago in his dream state and they appeared as cats. During the afternoon of that day, we had been out walking and stopped to talk to a neighbor's cat family. This lady had four cats of her own and she had also taken in four strays which people had left behind when they moved

152

(such cruelty). She had made warm winter quarters for them and fed them regularly and they came to love her. This was still foremost in our minds when we went to bed. The next morning, Geof announced he'd dreamed about six cats, two were standing on the side lines and the other four he couldn't control, because they kept hopping from one corner to another. They would wait for him to approach, then they would rush off and change corners laughing all the while. By this time in his narrative, I was laughing, knowing full well he'd met the Archangels and their two Watchers (guardians against negative forces which do exist in the Planes). Depending on what has last made a deep impression on your mind before you go to bed (or in your meditation), if they are feeling playful, they'll play games with you and you'll have to figure it out. When they are feeling communicative, they will take you to see the twelve gates of the zodiacal signs behind which are seventy two more Angels who work under the auspices of the Angels of the Zodiac.

Once again, we leave you to prepare yourself for this Mind Walk into the Archetypal Plane where you have a choice of meeting some of our own Inner Planes Group, the Angels of the Outer Planets or the Archangels. So take your time and "let Angels guide you on your lofty quest" as poet John Milton suggested.

Chapter 12
The Labyrinth, the EL, and the 5th Dimension

I f you found the other chapters fascinating when you took your Mind Walks, this one will captivate you. Again we reiterate, it's not easy. Getting the hang of moving into the EL and taking yourself into the 5th dimension really takes a mind shift. Once again, perseverance is the name of the game and the game is very rewarding. So let's take the easy one first and create a labyrinth (a sort of maze), where you can eventually find the center of yourself. Once you have found this jewel, this center, the Universe with all its Planes, Dimensions and spirits from other planets is literally your oyster. You will have freed yourself from the boundaries of this earthly reality, recognizing its illusiveness, and many out-of-body experiences are awaiting you.

Now, as we know, a garden maze created by human hands is a complex puzzle. Once entered, you have to find your way out again. If you take a wrong turn, you can go around in circles until you find the right exit. Many human beings lives are still like that. But you will not get lost within the creation of your own maze, because you have now trained yourself to become controller over your own self.

The maze you are going to construct in your mind will gently take you from the outside of yourself, moving path-by-path into the very core of your being. You will eventually understand the complex puzzle of your inner self.

You've done a great deal of work in finding yourself throughout the chapters of this book. What you consider at this moment to be

155

the "whole" you, now must continue to discover its parts and fully co-ordinate them. What you will be tapping into are the hidden depths and byways of the unconscious mind. These usually remain hidden behind the scenes for most people.

We are actually multi-dimensional creatures, although most may not recognize ourselves as such. The paths in the labyrinth that you are creating will connect you to portions of your different selves. This will propel you into other dimensions, bringing further enlightenment of the connectedness of everything in the Universe.

This spiritual journey marks a major turning point for you. It's a transitional stage between this physical world we tend to think of as reality and the deeper understanding of Universal togetherness. Here you will touch what Carl Jung described as the "Collective Unconscious" absorbing the energy patterns of cosmic unity: what you have been, what you are and what you will become.

Do you recall in chapter 4 we mentioned "reaching for your true self?" This is a continuation of that search, and this Mind Walk you will take into the labyrinth, will bring you face to face with your Shadow Self. For some, again, it can be a painful experience as you will be seeing yourself as you really are. Those portions of yourself which you have not wanted to previously recognize, have come home to roost. Your worst faults and weaknesses stand in front of you rather like a policeman blocking your path. Don't panic or feel ashamed. Take a good look at them and then see another portion of your Shadow Self. This will allow you to view parts of your potential which you've never developed; perhaps not even recognized as such.

This walk is the journey of your soul. Wherever your ideals are at this moment, is where you belong. The labyrinth will lead you into your own spiritual center and you will not return the way you entered. Insights and discoveries take place within the labyrinth of self leading to a sense of wholeness and balance.

Prepare yourself now to create your labyrinth. While you are thinking about it, you may do this in your mind or draw it first on a piece of paper. But you will be using it in your mind when you start to take your Mind Walk. Now, within the shape and size of your choice of labyrinth should be three separate important paths. You may choose as many paths as you wish in which to wander, but these three are very special. Make one path going directly up through the center of the labyrinth and the other two branching off, one to the left and the other to the right. The other paths you choose to put in to wander may be any shape and go any place – they are not important. But you should start off on one of them while you are adjusting your mind. Put a small flag at your starting point. In your mind, picture something or place you've been before or that you know well. Put as much detail in your mind picture (as you've done before) and use it as your jumping off point. Now, move forward on your chosen path (not the three important ones). And if you walk far enough, you'll pop out somewhere else into whatever place happens to be in your mind at the time, even if it's only in your subconscious. You will or should experience this with all your sharpened inner senses. Rather neat, don't you think?

Now, having got the hang of that, mentally make your way back to the important path which leads off to the left. Step firmly onto it, and as you make your way along the path, notice that you are moving in a spiral fashion going around and around to the left. This is a time spiral where you are unwinding time. Watch the changes that are taking place in the scenery and recognize that you are slowly moving backwards in time. You will find yourself looking back at life's experiences and the karmic choices of long, long ago. Gazing down the ages, you will have a much greater understanding of the actions and reactions that we had mentioned briefly in chapter 2. Here is your shadow self/dark side, the opposite of who you've always thought you were, showing itself to you through all your incarnations. You will see things that will make you shudder and you'll wonder how you could have been so callous. You will absorb the sense of the hurts you had forced on others. But as you watch, remember these are bygones. Here, you are the sum total of all your experiences from the beginning of time. It's an accumulation of selves past and present and shortly you will see your future. Note as you watch the continual habit patterns that you've brought with you into each one of your incarnations. Sir Herbert Read, in his book "Icon and Idea", put forward the theory that every kind of pattern is a form of thought and corresponds to an intelligible mental concept. As we said earlier on, thoughts become things and things become habit patterns which make us comfortable, or so we think. So study and analyze those patterns, follow the mental trends and recognize what you have brought with you this time. Where do they lead? Do you need them? Are they valuable or should you dispense with them?

Many years ago, Louis said to a class, "For although no incident which is in the past can affect the future, our thoughts impressed on the cells of our body can indeed affect us. We are as we think, and this is the only time a past action can have an effect on a future path – for the reaction of the whole 'I' is built on what has been impressed before."

This walk you are taking in the labyrinth is in search of the whole 'I'. What you are experiencing now should be a fascination, not a reaction. Do not let the Dweller on the Threshold (the lurking negative ego) impress any guilt on you; otherwise, you will fail this test of finding your true self.

Adjust your mind a little to the right to another portion of your shadow self and view that hidden potential which is now coming into view. Now, isn't that a glorious feature to behold? There is so much there that you have never been aware of. Some is brought forward from ages past which has never been put into operation. Some in this incarnation, you have shied away from because you felt you couldn't handle it. Now, with the cosmic energy of power you absorbed from the Archetypal Plane from your previous Mind Walk, you will be able to do anything you wish with the potential that is being shown to you. Absorb as much as you wish of this experience until you are ready to move on again.

Turn now and make your way back down this path, winding up time, considering what you have just seen and understood. Cross the center path and walk towards the right hand path where you can experience the future development of your creative potential.

As you mentally step onto this new spiral path, view this positive creativity. Keep moving through the spiral, always to the right, winding up time. Then out of this abundance, select what you wish to do, to become, to attain. Let your range of vision soar into the future. Not only in the world you now inhabit but way up into the future, generations ahead. Will you be incarnating again so far ahead? Ask your soul, it knows. Then you can decide what you will create, when and how and for what purpose. See yourself in your creation in as much detail as possible. Create it the way you wish it to be. And do not, we repeat, do not, for one moment, doubt anything you are creating. You are the Creator, remember that! Whatever you are developing will come to pass without any further help from you. Just vividly create your picture. Feel it, experience it, absorb the excitement of it. Then go away and leave it to get on with itself. Any time you wish to make further use of your potential of any sort, you now know how to get on with it. Keep in the forefront of your mind that you can do anything and achieve anything, because of your new found strength of will. Always remember that visualization is the corridor to your inner resources where potential and abilities come alive.

Having set things up for yourself, move back along the path and be prepared to walk the center. This is a marvelous walk. As you step onto this center path, everything you have seen and done in your meanderings through the portions of your labyrinth will fill you with a euphoria and enlightenment you have never felt before. This is truly spiritual enlightenment.

Vivid colors, glowing lights, crystalline rocks amongst the moving trees, pulsing with their own internal light will greet you as you move into this wonderland. Look also at yourself and you will discover that you, too are composed of frequencies of light. Can you hear your own musical soul notes? We are also composed of sound as well as color, a vibratory energy which interacts with everything else in the Universe. Time and space no longer exist for you now and you will be enveloped by an all-encompassing feeling of love, peace and serenity.

Further down the path, you will come across a beautiful gazebo where you may sit and contemplate. Imagine a garden of crystal and silver leaves so thin they transmit light. Now, imagine drawing a violin bow across this petrified time bringing forth the music of the spheres, which can be seen as a rainbow of hues/notes and heard as a shower of crystal petals which you can now absorb into the very fiber of your soul.

Surrounded by flowers, animals who will greet and sit with you, and this rainbow of such beauty arched above you, you will see and feel within the center of yourself the wholeness and oneness of everything. Sloughing of your skin will take place until you feel the slenderness of the Universal web entwined within you and you will know, without a doubt, that you have discovered the parts of yourself that truly make up the real whole self. Your many sides have finally become integrated.

Having found your whole self, focus on the near distance and you will see the black and white pillars of Boaz and Joachim with the Temple Veil stretched between them. How will you rend that Veil and meet the Ones behind the backdrop? Chapter 13 will take you there, but in the meantime, learn to utilize this Mind Walk and take advantage of the content of your labyrinth.

With the personal knowledge you have just encountered in your Mind Walk in the labyrinth, you have released your soul from the chains of illusion of this earthly plane. Unfettered at last, it will certainly "fly high" to other dimensions, other universes. How about other galaxies where you can watch baby stars being born on a daily basis so the old stars can get some rest and discover their old soul energy. When you see the stardust, this is just the beginning. Watch and you will see them coagulate, then become energy balls and ultimately, souls. (Even stars have a consciousness.) There are always millions being born. Time after time, the stars wink out in one area and glow in a new one, dashing like a wave of stardust in glimmering profusion. That's the way of the Universe. You don't believe? Just wait until you take a walk up the EL.

You are not the first nor will you be the last to experience these and other wonders. The ECK Masters have been traveling in and out of their bodies for thousands of years. So have the twelfth century Persian Sufis (who also knew that through visualization they could alter and reshape the fabric of their destiny – just what you have been learning through this book), Yogis, Shamans, the Amazon Indians, Madame Blavatsky, W. C. Leadbeater (a disciple of hers), Padre Pio, an Italian Capuchin Monk and Swedish mystic Swedenborg. We could go on for pages about the people who have experienced these other realms and they all spout similar descriptions. For instance, being able to see in all directions at once, being in two or more places at once (at one time I found myself walking up a straight path, but I also met myself at the same time coming back on the other side of me, rather like a divided highway). Others include conversing with Angels and spirits, seeing landscapes so beautiful no words can describe them, dazzling light giving out feelings of love, peace and serenity, and at the same time, knowing that time and space no longer exist. Emmanuel Swedenborg had so many mystical visions in his later life that he produced twenty volumes describing them and his works inspired many authors and poets, particularly William Blake. But it is now high time for you to find out for yourself that these other realms really do exist.

Prepare yourself to travel the EL and that's exactly what it will look like in your mind; the letter L. We don't have to remind you now of your quiet place and the White Light. It should be automatic whenever you do your spiritual work. So imagine now that you are standing inside an elevator, but mentally move it sideways first until it comes to a stop and then move it upwards. Scientists say that imaginary time is a mathematical concept. They say it is the direction of time at right angles to real time. But what is real time or imaginary time? By walking the EL, you are moving at right angles and this is where five dimensions meet; where the up is time and the down is energy.

In one of my walks in the EL, I had a fascinating experience. I could see the colors and shapes of an indescribable world. The colors of the rainbow, but much more intense. I couldn't decide whether I was trying to photograph it or capture it in paint on a canvas. I was also surrounded by music which vibrated in color, yet I seemed to be able to taste it. There was so much activity going on, I had trouble recording it in my mind/dream state. I finally discussed it with Louis to see if he could sort it out, and this was his reply: "Pity about the lost struggle to transfer Inner Plane stuff into the material world. Certainly the all-pervading, single sense experience of anything in the Planes just gets distorted when it's broken up and allocated to the various separate physical senses. It's rather like a jigsaw puzzle which, when completed, is appreciated by eye, ear, nose, tongue and hand simultaneously. Consequently, the original picture (experience rather) is only approachable when you can see with your ears, listen with your tongue and so forth. From our side here within the Planes, these five dimensions seem to draw solid pyramids on one-dimensional surfaces, where thought comes in king-size packages, weighable and measurable in profundity and significance. Harmony makes music you can feel with your eyes, savor with your nose and touch with your ears. We can build a symphony four ways from a point, creating a holy architecture which is the stairway to paradise. We can also communicate by seven-sense one-ness to the souls around us and use the energy exchange to propel at thrice light towards the Source, where inverse cube law develops a widening spiral of energy to focus the effort. Here, I struggle with words to describe the ineffable, but it's the sort of experience you encounter when you travel the EL." A somewhat enigmatic experience which we can look forward to.

Now, provided you get off on the correct line, you can go galaxy hopping or any other travel you wish. There are more than five dimensions. Science talks about the eleven they have found, but, say our "boys" in their reality, there are hundreds to be investigated and science will be a long while catching up with them.

It's not easy to walk the EL. Before I had that interesting happening which I've just described, I battled for a long time in my meditations before I complained bitterly to Louis that I was getting nowhere, just ending up with a load of frustration. His reply was, "The higher you take your mind into the Planes, the less memory you're likely to bring back, as there seems to be no satisfactory symbols to fit into your dreams or meditations to represent what you've experienced. Only through the changes in your material world, will you recognize your achievement." Certainly, my material world was constantly changing, but this didn't pacify me at all. He said, "Memory can be made to retain that which it is not designed by evolution to record." "A trick which will work," he says, "is to capture the first awakening thought of the new day and pass (in thought) back along the silver cord to the preceding thought. If the process is not overlain with spurious experiences of sleep engendered by the subconscious stirring, one can dive below the surface of mind/memory and obtain impressions of the soul flights along the EL." It can be done he says, especially if one stills the mind with meditation as a prelude to slipping directly from the meditational state into sleep.

This worked for me, for it usually takes me quite a while to drop off to sleep. Now, when I want to take a walk along the EL, I sit up in bed amongst a load of fat pillows and meditate there. First, I relax. Then I take my attention gradually up my body from my feet, visualizing all the while the opening in my skull through which I will move my consciousness. This is a very ancient method used by the Masters of long ago and passed on to their chelas. In fact, Pythagoras, who was well versed in the mysteries of the Magi, instructed his students to go out through the top of the head, stating that this is the point with which the human self merges with the spirit. Louis taught me this exercise way back in 1969, and I use it feeling my inner self gradually moving upwards. Then, I allow myself to slip into sleep (on my pillows) and take off onto the EL, most times bringing back memories, or partial memories. This is how I am able to share my experiences of the birth of stars with you.

This one was an interesting walk along the EL where Louis and I seemed to be interpreting musical notes from flowers. He suggested we were visiting the Pi-Zeta-Epsilon planets where the inhabitants have an incredible (to us) range of senses. Their rainbow breaks down not into seven colors like ours, but some fifteen thousand shades, all of which they can distinguish. Consequently, they use colors instead of letters and words as a written language. They showed us their very pretty books. Their ears can distinguish a change in pitch of a hemi-demi-semi-semi-semi quaver, which makes our eight note scale split up into about two thousand separate notes. Sound, in the sense of music, is used as communication, including their poetry which sounds like a chime of faerie bells.

I was pulling all this together, holding tightly to the images when the phone rang. Unfortunately, I had forgotten to switch it off the night before and, would you believe, it was a wrong number! I've had many other interesting and fascinating excursions and so will you, if this is what you would like to experience. It will just take some working on to be able to achieve it.

If you are not getting anywhere in your usual meditational state, try this system, it may well work for you, too. But don't battle with it, it's merely another interesting walk in the Planes. Lack of accomplishment in this area will not detract from the continuation of your spiritual journey. In fact, you will immensely enjoy this next journey in the following chapter. Finally, after all your hard work, you are about to visit the City of Serenity, meet the Lords of Flame and others, and experience your major initiation. Are you ready for the next adventure of your spiritual journey?

Chapter 13
The City of Serenity, The Lords,
The Temple of Wisdom, Your Initiation

We frequently find that spiritually inclined people tend to avoid cities as much as possible. The noise, smells and vibrations pound into our heads and climb up our spines, upsetting our equilibrium. We're usually glad to get home again into our own peaceful surroundings. This City of Serenity, next on your agenda, is one visit which will enthrall you, and you will want to visit as often as possible.

You are now approaching the summit to which this book has been guiding you. Your welcoming committee consists of the remaining seven Lords of Karma, the seven Lords of Flame, the Lords of the twelve Rays and they who are simply called The Nameless Ones (the over-lords of the ones just mentioned). These Nameless Ones will be conducting your initiation.

At the entrance to the city, is a Beacon which focuses its light of purification on the entrants, encouraging a feeling of bliss and serenity to infiltrate the soul.

Within the city, stands the Hall of Learning. You've been in the Hall many times. This is where the flowing thoughts of the teachers and masters become discourses which all Chelas interpret and absorb into their own level of understanding. Whatever is needed, is there. Whatever the soul requires. Reunions and peace are frequent themes. As are the replacing of cracked ideals, cleaning the windows of the souls and minds or knocking out dents in battered psyches. There is also a special section there in which our Peter radiates peace and harmony for those who are ready to receive.

In recent years, the Hall has become quite populated. As more and more of the gold robed Ascended Masters are now "materializing" around this center of power, part of the area itself has become a City of Resting for them. Our Peter and Darius (mentioned earlier) have taken up "residence" there and have dubbed it the City of Serenity. Again, I battle with words – these blunt tools – to try to describe the nothingness, but the everything of the focus of energy.

Let's try this one again and try to draw a word picture which your inner mind can absorb, then you'll know what to expect when you visit. Now, Peter, in *his* consciousness (remember you take your consciousness with you when you die?) resides in a stone and timber dwelling in the East of the City. Within the Planes, there is no up, down or sideways, so Peter's residence is a place for him to focus on – or to "be"– such that he has a spatial reference instead of a multi-dimensional non-reference. In order to have meaning to one's self, it is necessary to have a mental anchor point – and that, to the inhabitant, appears as a residence in the Planes.

If we may backtrack for the moment and perhaps make things a little clearer? In our earlier chapters, we talked about having many dimensions within ourselves. In actual fact, these dimensions are really densities of energy. The slower the energy vibrates, the more solid and dense things seem to be. This is the reason people who are not interested in metaphysical/mystical things see only this material solid plane and they react to whatever is going on around them. Now, as you have been learning to take control of yourself, when you meditate and get deep down within, your energy level vibrates faster and faster and you leave the density of the physical level. You are ceasing to see it, but experiencing other frequencies – other dimensions vibrating at different speeds. Your own material earth plane is still here, but you are experiencing other worlds, other existences.

If this is not quite clear to you, here is another simple example. Think of the radio and television stations which are broadcasting all day. All are on different frequencies, yet all of them are occupying the same space, as well as occupying the same space you are in. When you change channels, the one you've been listening to or watching doesn't stop. It still exists as before, but you are no longer tuned into its frequency. This is what happens to you when you are meditating, doing spiritual exercises which increase your vibration, or you experience inner plane activity within your dreams. Wherever you take your consciousness during your meditation period (or whichever chapter you happen to be working with), you've "changed channels" and are experiencing another program.

When you reach this level of frequency of the City of Serenity, you will see these buildings/residences of those who occupy this space at the time they need it when they come to lecture, to listen and absorb from others whose wisdom and knowledge is higher than theirs. Or when they need to utilize the healing shrines when they suffer an energy depletion. When they return to their own frequency level, their residence is no longer there. That space is occupied by something else.

Perhaps you can understand now that as you move your consciousness into these different frequencies, more and more of these higher levels are an invisible force, and what you are really in touch with, is the ascension of a spiritual principle. Here is the group mind of Angels in the Inner Planes. So it is vitally important that you employ symbols, color, music and strong visualization in how you expect to "see" them to make this connection. Together, this group forms an idea and activates the force to bring it to fruition in the form requested.

This of course, is what you will do when you prepare yourself to take this very special Mind Walk towards your major initiation. You will remember to do your relaxation, White Light and your walk through the gate first, won't you? Then, along with your color and music, visualize your Star Wand as the symbol to propel yourself forward into the Temple of Wisdom. This is your first stop before entering the Hall of Initiation. You see, the stylized shape of the symbols identify or attach themselves to the area of the Astral Plane you are working with; whereby, you obtain some knowledge across the unseen to use in the seen (your physical plane). Now, in this Plane, when the symbols are engraved on your mind so powerfully, you are connected through the Veil of the Temple. The clearing and sweeping of your channel with the correct vibration (i.e. color, music, symbol, incense), opens the door to let the Light of the Temple fall across the threshold of your mind. We suggest now that you finish reading this chapter first, then everything will come together in your mind before you take your Walk.

What else are you going to find within this glorious Plane? Well, we mentioned the four Arch Angels before and they hold dominion here over the Quarters. The Hall, being at the center, makes up the fifth point. Now, twelve rays, representing the Lords of the Rays, radiate from the Hall like spokes of a wheel (or the cusps of an astrological chart). Then each of the four Angels has dominion over three signs. Along the appropriate rays "live" the Masters, so the whole "place" is like a city. In fact, at a certain distance from the Hall and the Beacon, the rays undergo a metamorphosis making twelve doors through which to enter the city. And the doors are guarded overall by the Arch Angels, and they have sub-Arch Angels (one level below them) who look after each door. Behind each door, as you will eventually find, are a further seventy two Angels. If you are into astrology, you will

170

recognize that the seventy two represent each side of each decanate of the signs.

Let's move on now to describe the Temple of Wisdom which is the outer portion of where your initiation will take place. Inside the Temple, is the white Altar surrounded by the Thrones of the lesser gods. Before them are the two pillars of Boaz and Joachim, the silver and black, that we mentioned in chapter 12. Slung between them hangs the Veil of the Temple and below the Veil are the black and white checkered squares of the Temple floor. Symbolically it represents the universe which we inhabit. The Veil of the Temple should be considered to be the forces, force fields, focuses of energy that make up the whole of this universe. One pillar, the black one on the left (when you are facing them), represents this material plane and the other silver one represents the upper end of the spiritual planes. Remember, this Veil is made of energies, a web of energies, and at certain points within this web, the energies become coherent and measurable by the soul body combination of a human being. It's an organization of energies, a negative space around which we give form to ourselves.

Part of the left hand side of the Veil includes all of the physical phenomena of physical body, earth, stars, moon, comets. In fact, all the things you own which are only made of circulating atoms, are all organized energy and part of the same web or Veil of the Temple.

Now, move across the web a little to the right, and towards the silver pillar. You immediately leave the material (let's call them knots) and come in contact with more ethereal knots of energy. These are the mental energies and in a band there within the Veil exists mental, emotional and soul energies of we human beings, animals, trees – anything which has an aura – which is everything. And the further to the right you go, the more the energy is etherealized. These focuses (knots) in the net become the Angels, entities, gods, and beings, complete with body, mind emotion and soul.

So, going from the left to the right, these energies intermingle and the Veil of the Temple is merely being a web of energies suspended between the two pillars. If it was not for either or both of these pillars, this universe would not exist. So the material is as important to the spiritual, as the spiritual is to the material. They both must exist as two poles must exist to a battery. If a unipolar system of anything was produced, it would merely be a scientific curiosity because it would have no dynamism, no power to do anything, because there would be no power for cancellation or for flow. Therefore, we have the two pillars and the Veil.

Down below, at right angles to the Veil is the checkered floor board. That beautifully polished non-slippery checker board of black and white squares. Black ones symbolize material and white ones symbolize total spirituality. There are no gray squares on the floor of the Temple – merely two extremes, because whoever walks on that floor is filling the space between the white and the black. It is undesirable to walk only on one square for any length of time. Walking purely on the black squares, you will be weighed down with the materiality of this world.

Unfortunately, it is quite easy to walk only on one square of the Temple. It is undesirable from the point of your own evolution and power, because if you walk only on the black square, that square will demand white power to make an energy flow. The very act of treading across all black squares will draw all your spiritual power into your feet. It drains your spiritual energy in the most literal sense of the word, because black is only doing its job of looking for an energy flow. So whatever white energy you have inside yourself, will be sucked out by using only the black squares and there you have a rather unpleasant imbalance. Recall the unbalanced force we mentioned in chapter seven?

So now we have a solidly material entity without the balancing flow of spiritual energy and if you go far enough into the Temple in this material state, you will come to a halt. Rather like a battery which has run down, there is no exchange of energy. So there you stand, a fully material being and along comes the cosmic vacuum cleaner and whips away this material energy – so, no entry into the Hall of Initiation. And similarly, if you walk only on the white squares, you will find they are thirsty for material power. So this material energy will be drawn from you, and you'll end up with a useless puddle of spiritual power. You'll be totally immobile on a white square somewhat further up the Temple towards the Great Throne. You'll be unable to move because you do not have a balancing flow. Once again, the "Lords of the Vacuum Cleaners" will come along and remove it, so don't play lions and tigers on the squares. Walk straight up the middle on an equal number of black and white squares, absorbing positive and negative energy, which will enable you to continue towards the Throne where you are going.

That's how we all make symbolic progress, and that's why there is always strong teaching, understanding and strong presentation of the value of both material and spiritual imbalance. This has nothing to do with being godly or ungodly. This balance keeps the engine or machine (which is you) running that focus of energy, which is the real you.

Having understood now how the energy flow works, you should be ready to take your Mind Walk into the Temple in preparation for your major initiation. Do you recall within the latter stage of your walk in the Labyrinth, you saw in the distance, the Pillars of Boaz and Joachim holding the Temple Veil between them? If you have assessed yourself and your soul correctly and balanced your energy patterns, you will find yourself walking the black and white squares towards them. Step across the threshold of the Temple, breathe deeply, view your surroundings and make your obeisance to the lesser gods. If you are correct in the judgment of yourself, the Veil of the Temple will rend and disappear, and in that moment you will have recognition and acceptance of the world of illusion; fully understanding that you create your own world by the power of your thoughts.

As the Veil drops, the principal gods will appear and you will be ushered forward by your Angels into the Hall of Initiation. To experience the magic of this happening on this Plane is most surely a divine process of spiritual development.

Standing between your Angels, look up and see the sparkling white pillars towering, with the gold lattice between them and the shining white marble of the floor. Flanked on each side are the crystal thrones, each with its god. See now He with the head of a bird, He who holds the Ankh, He who sits beneath the golden lotus – and the others – rank upon serried rank of They. Far, far along the mighty Hall until at the end, you see a larger Throne and a light which makes the sun seem like an extinguished candle. Yet it will not hurt your eyes. These are the Lords of Flame, the Lords of Karma, the Lords of the Twelve Rays and others you will meet shortly. At this point, I must mention that the description of the gods is how I have always seen them, and I am now describing to you my own major initiation which took place in November 1970. Your mind may, and probably will, interpret them in a totally different way.

To continue this description of an initiation, you will hear the music of the throbbing of ten million souls who have been invited. You will smell the incense smoking up from the thuribles and runcible spoons. As the spiritual Sun arises, the planets and their Angels sing in mighty chorus. Having moved forward towards the Great Throne you will wonder who that is lying totally still upon the marble floor with the gods frozen as if carved from solid light. You are actually standing outside yourself at this moment. Then the form lifts itself, raises its arms - and it is *YOU.*

The gods spring to their feet in unison and the very Cosmos trembles with this shout of welcome. A paean of praise arises and you walk through the lines of Thrones, taking power here, a cleansing there and you stand, dwarfed by the Light, before the Nameless Ones. The Wand and Sword touch and the scene pinwheels into a bright effulgence of the Oneness of Being.

You will now be given your Astral Name, but be very careful with whom you share it. Names are power as we mentioned before and the knowledge of a name gives power over its owner. Hence – Angels really have no names, so you cannot have power over them. They merely respond to the image you have visualized to which you have given energy and form. The Angels do not pronounce their names for fear of Astral reprisals. If you called them by their own names, you would change *their* Karmic pattern which is why you will never know what they are really called. Neither does it matter what name you have been given to call them – they will know when they are needed.

This is your major initiation. Just as the physical earth drama is observed by the Angels, the Watchers and the Lords, they in turn, are watched by their own Lords, Watchers and Angels. Somewhere beyond our conception, a cosmic audience watches what goes on within this mighty sphere. And as you gaze into the distance behind the Lords and the Nameless Ones, you will perceive the essence of the Old gods. If you are very lucky, beyond the Old gods, you may catch a sensation of the Ultra Terrestrials, who are of course, the gods of the gods.

Blessed Be.

The Tide of Divine Union

Thou seekest in the timorous mind - a touch, no more - yet
Less and more than words do pass between thee.
Even as the creaming breakers flood the conscious mind
Then shall ye know in the last reckoning
In the cold clear light of reason swamping all
Logic, ties nor family
Shall stand against this tide.
Deep swells the pending union
And deeper thrusts the knife of a new and stranger pulling
A heart and mind encounter
Crashing like a sunburst
Outwards upwards inwards outwards
Until the carnate beings dwell in splendor on a lonely cloud
Beyond the tiny roils of earth
Tis to be, even as I say
Try as ye may - but with each dawning day
The straining waters lap against the dam
Which, breaking of a sudden,
Sweeps all away
To leave but driftwood jetsam
And the words
I - thou.

By
Lt. Louis F. Hellerman W.W. One Fighter Pilot

Born December 24, 1898. Shot down in flames August 15, 1917.

Given to us by automatic writing August, 1971.

About the Author

An executive of The Hermetic Order of Campo Santo, a mystery school in Canada, Maiya Gray-Cobb was born in Kent, England and is currently living in Melfort, Saskatchewan with her husband, Geof Gray-Cobb. She was educated at Brantridge Forest University and has earned a Ph.D. in parapsychology. Her mystical path has taken her to Spain, the U.S., South Africa and Canada and her work, lectures and seminars have appeared in numerous places in the world.

Certainly this book will be a rewarding experience to readers in Maiya's newest work which has so many dimensions and great substance.

Other Books Published
by
Ozark Mountain Publishing, Inc.

PO Box 754
Huntsville, AR 72740
www.ozarkmt.com
1-800-935-0045/479-738-2348 Wholesale Inquiries Welcome